Music and People with Developmental Disabilities

Music Therapy, Remedial Music Making and Musical Activities

of related interest

Music Therapy in Health and Education
Edited by Margaret Heal and Tony Wigram
Foreword by Anthony Storr
ISBN 1 85302 175 X

The Music Has Spoken For Us
Clinical Improvisational Studies in Adult Psychiatry
Julienne Cartwright
ISBN 1 85302 259 4

'Here-and-Now Music Therapy'
Experimental Music Improvisation with Dementia Sufferers
Julienne Cartwright
ISBN 1 85302 258 6 pb
ISBN 1 85302 260 8 Video

Making Music with the Young Child with Special Needs
A Guide for Parents
Elaine Streeter
ISBN 1 85302 187 3

Music and People with Developmental Disabilities

Music Therapy, Remedial Music Making and Musical Activities

Frans Schalkwijk

Translated by Andrew James

Jessica Kingsley Publishers
London and Bristol, Pennsylvania

First published in the Netherlands as
Muziek in de Hulpverlening aan Geestelijk Gehandicapten
by Uitgeverij INTRO, Nijerk, The Netherlands

First published in English in the United Kingdom in 1994 by
Jessica Kingsley Publishers Ltd
116 Pentonville Road
London N1 9JB, England
and
1900 Frost Road, Suite 101
Bristol, PA 19007, U S A

Library of Congress Cataloging in Publication Data
Schalkwijk, F.W. (Frans W.)
Music and people with developmental disabilities: music therapy
remedial music making, and musical activities / F.W. Schalkwijk.
128p. cm.
Includes bibliographical references
ISBN 1-85302-226-8
1. Music therapy. 2. Mentally handicappe--Education--Music
I. Title
ML3920.S323 1994
616.85'88065154--dc20

British Library Cataloguing in Publication Data
Schalkwijk, F.W.
Music and People with Developmental Disabilities
Music Therapy, Remedial Music Making and Musical Activities
I. Title
615.85154

ISBN 1-85302-226-8

Printed and Bound in Great Britain by
Biddles Ltd., Guildford and King's Lynn

Contents

I dedicate this book to Jair and Mishka, the two little brothers who were never allowed to play on the computer where the strange characters used to pop up, which you now see before you. For the time being I don't need the computer, so...

Amsterdam, May 1988

The realization of this book was made possible through the financial support granted by the Netherlands Comité Kinderpostzegels and by the Hogeschool Nijmegen who supported the translation.

Preface

In November 1987 my doctoral thesis, entitled 'Music Therapy with the Mentally Handicapped', was presented in Leuven. In it, an account was given of a study conducted into the practice of music therapy with people with developmental disabilities in the Netherlands. The study was carried out between 1983 and 1987. The thesis explains how, in practice, music therapists work at child day care centres, adult day care centres and other institutions. They were asked, with the help of an extensive questionnaire, to describe their own working methods. A large number of music therapists took part in the study. In the study report the planning, completion, numerical calculations of the data and the results were comprehensively reproduced, including the most detailed points, which would be tiresome to readers who do not feel comfortable with research jargon. Therefore, this book contains an abridged version of the study report, in which the research jargon has been left out. A concise description of the way in which the study was carried out is provided in the Appendix.

In addition to the obvious similarities (as regards content) between the original thesis and this book, there are indisputable differences. In the thesis, the results were described just as they emerged in the study. In this book the results have been interpreted more freely, in keeping with the practice of music therapy. For this reason, case studies have been included and I have endeavoured to give a theoretical basis to the results of the study. In this sense, this book is more than just the original report; it is a mixture of study reports and interpretation by the author.

The contents of this book are, in brief, as follows. First of all, a very concise outline of the historical developments of music therapy with people with developmental disabilities is given. Then a more theoretical chapter follows in which different ways of caring for people through the medium of music-making are described. The main body of the book is devoted to a discussion of these various methods, including individual treatment and group treatment. Each method is described in the light of the symptoms shown, the objectives set and the choice of techniques and musical instruments. Putting this into daily practice is made clear by presenting (fictitious) case studies. In the fifth and final chapter, individual annotations are included from the study and theoretical conclusions drawn.

The scope of the book lies within clear boundaries. One of the reasons for this is that good publications are already available on this subject. This book is limited to providing the beginnings of a methodical synthesis of indications, objectives and techniques. One consequence of this is that this book hardly gives any description of how the music therapist makes music and what rhythms, types of beat, keys, tempos, and so forth he chooses. First, this was not examined in the study, and there is still little systematic knowledge about it. Second, it is not my goal to present the reader with a 'recipe book'.

There are two things I would like to draw to your attention.

The first is the question of word usage. I have opted for the term developmental disability; however, I do not attach any particular significance to this, in the sense of imparting one specific under-standing as to the nature of the disabilities. In choosing other terms, it was really a matter of giving careful thought as to the content. I am of the opinion that a music therapist, caring for people with developmental disabilities, belongs to the category known as expert, and for this reason I will refer to him or her as a music therapist, irrespective of whether he is called 'Andy' or 'Sarah' or the 'music maestro' in his institution. Anyone who comes to the music therapist for expert help, I call in this book a client, irrespective of whether she or he is known as a resident, pupil, child, and so forth in the institution. In everyday language used in the institutions, this is in fact not common practice, but it will leave us in no doubt as to the type of relationship between the music therapist and the other person. There is one person who is requesting help, and there is one person who is offering to give help. Both of them are of equal worth to one another, but their relationship, in a caring situation, is unequal.

Many terms also exist in practice for what the music therapist does. Music therapy is used as a generic term, covering an extremely diverse range of working methods. In the first chapter of the book, current language usage is examined. As from the second chapter, in which different types of care are described, I make a more specific distinction. In order to attain conceptual clarity, the use of the word 'therapy' from this point onwards is reserved for compound forms such as in the terms 'music therapy' and 'psychotherapy'. As we will see in Chapter Two, music therapy refers to something other than a form of therapy used in conjunction with drug therapy, physio-therapy, cooking therapy, and so forth. For 'offering help', I make reference to the terms 'care' and 'treatment'. The point at which care starts and finishes is, in practice, not always a clear-cut matter. In this book the work of professional music therapists is set out and so the emphasis has been placed on care. I actually skirt around the discussion of what differences might exist between 'taking action' towards a client and 'treating' a client, as I do concerning the question of the place of education in taking action towards a client/treating a client.

Although it has emerged in the study that exactly half of the music therapists in the Netherlands are male, and consequently the other half are female, I have opted for the male form in gender denotations.

The second thing I would like to do is to express my thanks to all those who helped in the study. First, I am greatly indebted to Prof. Dr. Germain Lietaer and Prof. Dr. Marcel van Walleghem, who worked very closely with me as supervisor and co-supervisor in conducting my research. At different stages of the study, a number of music therapists and psychologists worked in close collaboration with me and gave me their support. For this, I am greatly thankful to the following colleagues: Loes Claerhoudt, Jack Dekker, Arnold Goedhardt, Meertine Laansma, Margreet Luikinga, Philip van Praag, Eugenie van Rest, Corrie Schalker and Frits Schoeren. Eugenie van Rest also read through the manuscript of this book, to make constructive contributions to it. I greatly appreciated her suggestions. A great number of other music therapists helped in the study by filling in a questionnaire and providing videos. Without their cooperation, this study would not have been possible.

The research was made possible with the help of a subsidy, granted by the BUMA-Fund for Music Therapy and the Nederlands Comité Kinderpostzegels and was given the administrative support of the Stichting Vrienden van Gehandicapten Amstelland en Meerlanden.

CHAPTER 1

The Use of Music in Caring for People with Developmental Disabilities

Introduction

The use of music in caring for people with developmental disabilities has a long tradition in the Netherlands. A first approach to this can be found in Lievgoed's doctoral thesis, 'Maat, Ritme en Melodie' ('Meter, Rhythm and Melody'), which came out in 1939.

In it he describes, from an anthroposophic point of view, his observations as to the musical opportunities open to people with developmental disabilities. After this book, nothing appeared for a long time. Nevertheless, new ground was broken in working with people with developmental disabilities by various individuals, these mainly being musicians. The books, for example, by Juliette Alvin, Paul Nordoff and Clive Robbins, which were published in English during the sixties, bear witness to this breakthrough. In the Netherlands, too, over the years, different work has been carried out on music therapy; however, very little has yet been written about it. Broadly speaking, it can be said that in this respect a change has come about since the mid-seventies. The subject began to grow beyond its infant stage. Although the books with a strong practical emphasis by the aforementioned pioneers in this subject remain of interest to all students, since then other publications have become available which also offer a theoretical perspective. The differences in understanding within this subject are becoming gradually more distinguishable and different schools of thought more apparent.

The first approach towards music therapy: occupational

For a long time, having a developmental disability was looked upon as synonymous with having a psychiatric illness. Anyone who was unable to carry on living at home with his parents was hidden away behind the closed doors of a psychiatric institution in the woods or by the sea. Because recovering from a developmental disability is simply not possible, relatively little care from those giving treatment was available to them. Pictures of spacious, lofty rooms where a large group of people with developmental disabilities would eat, 'live' and sleep, have still not completely gone out of circulation. People with a developmental disability were destined to live the life of an untouchable. Little by little, the thought emerged that in each case it would be a good thing to offer activities, such as walking, work therapy, music-making, and other such things. Activities such as singing in a choir, playing in a drum band or in an orchestra can always bring great pleasure and satisfaction.

The beginnings of the development of music therapy, leaving aside music therapy of an anthroposophic nature, can be traced back to this kind of activity. A pioneer English music therapist, Juliette Alvin, discovered that getting people with a developmental disability to watch and listen to her playing the cello evoked an enormous reaction. She used to visit them on the wards, make music to them, played different sorts of musical games with them and invited them at least to touch the cello for themselves to get a noise out of it. In this way they were stimulated, as well as being invited to take part in a pleasant activity. At about the same time, in America, Paul Nordoff and Clive Robbins were developing, in schools and day care centres for people with developmental disabilities, musical games in which each person, according to his own abilities, could make his own musical contributions. In this way each person got the chance to experience the pleasure of music.

In the Netherlands many music therapists also work on the basis of this tradition. The music therapist visits the ward or the community, taking an instrument for accompaniment so that they can sing along, as well as a few small percussion instruments for them to join in. In the book *De muziek waard* by Blatter, van Nunen and Verhoeven (1982), types of games using musical activities with people with developmental disabilities are described. The music therapist can even direct a choir, a pop group, an orchestra or a drum band. Playing in a drum band has become a tradition, especially in the South of the Netherlands. The Josti band is, more than any other, very well known in the Netherlands. Other possible activities open to the music therapist include working together on a radio or television programme, which is broadcast in the institution, or directing a Nativity play, for example. Some music therapists even give music lessons to people with a developmental disability; however, the area of music education is not touched upon in this book.

Music therapy as a form of care

The notion that having a developmental disability is synonymous with having a psychiatric illness is becoming obsolete. Having a developmental disability is seen more and more as a physically-induced limitation. The causes of developmental disability are extremely divergent, ranging from a genetic disorder to a physical illness, from toxaemia in pregnancy to a car accident. Although the disability itself is incurable, various faculties remain which, despite the limitations, can indeed be developed.

The search for new terminology bears out how a re-interpretation has been sought: the medical model is making way for a developmental model, in which the developmental disability is seen as a limiting factor in the possibilities for growth in mental development. When the development of a person with a developmental disability is retarded, seen from the point of view of what could normally be expected of the person, it is still possible to allow these faculties to develop with the help of special attention. Providing a suitable educational environment to stimulate growth is the aim of remedial education.

Besides these kinds of educational strategies, specialised strategies in caring for people with developmental disabilities have also been developed, which could best be adopted in special institutions for people with developmental disabilities. This approach resulted in an enormous boom in the numbers of child day care centres and adult day care centres over a short space of time. Music therapy was then also incorporated as a viable form of care.

At the end of the sixties, a number of movements came into being. One sizeable movement uses music as a means of practising certain skills. It was in this way that, in the Netherlands, Gretener-von Sury developed a method of stimulating various skills through music and movement, as well as developing the senses, concentration, the ability to cope with order, and so forth. Practising skills based on the musical–rhythmical aspects of music stands in stark contrast to many American methods. In America, music is commonly used as a form of reward: the behaviour called for by the music therapist is rewarded by allowing the person to listen to music, and unwanted behaviour can be curbed by depriving the person of a musical reward. In this way a pattern of behaviour resulting in self-injury, for example, can be broken, interactive skills taught and contact may even be established with an autistic child.

Another way to stimulate skills is to wrap up the 'subject matter' in a song. In the Netherlands, for example, Wim ter Burg has developed musical teaching aids, in which the days of the week are sung and thus learnt.

In these forms of music therapy, the emphasis is primarily laid upon the stimulation or teaching of skills, which are important to the person with a developmental disability in normal everyday life. Sometimes the skills are, unequivocally, of great importance to them; sometimes, however, they are clearly based on the standards and value systems of the non-developmentally disabled.

In the seventies another movement emerged, in which the accent shifted from practising skills to developing faculties which enable the person with a developmental disability to be himself and to express himself. In other words, more and more attention is being given to the individuality of people with developmental disabilities. The notion that a person with a developmental disability, like any other person, can fulfil their full potential in personal relationships with other people, is gaining more and more ground. The aforementioned school of thought, known as the 'relationship model', is being expressly adopted, particularly by the music therapists Remi Adriaansz and Loek Stijlen, as a form of care leading to self-realization and personal development. Other music therapists who have explicitly expressed their intentions to pursue this include, for example, Wim ter Burg, Paul Nordoff and Clive Robbins and Edith Boxill.

Music therapy as a form of psychotherapeutic care

Now that more consideration has been given to the opportunities for development open to a person with a developmental disability, more consideration is also being given to the causes of this kind of developmental pattern, which has, in the course of time, been interrupted or retarded, although opportunities still appear to be exploitable. On the one hand, aspects of development are related to one another and established gaps in development, known as an 'imbalanced developmental profile', constitute grounds for considering care. On the other hand, slowly but surely, more attention is being devoted to the specific psychological problems of people with developmental disabilities. After all, the more that individuality is emphasised, the more the individual, specific problems will be identified. People with a developmental disability undergo psychosocial development as well and they too can experience problems in this (quite outside of their retardation, caused by the developmental disability, and their developmental limitations). These kind of problems can manifest themselves in the form of behavioural disturbances, neurotic complaints or psychiatric symptoms.

Discerning psychological problems in people with developmental disabilities is a very recent undertaking and the development of methods in music therapy is just as recent in origin. Nevertheless, many music therapists are of the opinion that music therapy can be reliably used as a form of psychotherapy. Initiatives in this are being seen in the Netherlands, amongst other places. Already in various publications, Eugenie van Rest and Remi Adriaansz and Loek Stijlen have suggested adopting music therapy in this way. Stijlen (1984) described a similar form of music therapy with a young woman who, amongst other things, was suffering from an identity crisis. Up to now there have been all too few descriptions of forms of 'music psychotherapy' with people with developmental disabilities written up.

Conclusion

In the chapters to follow, all the trends in music therapy quoted above will be examined in more detail. In Chapter Two, the three different forms of music therapy (activities, practice, psychotherapy) will come under extensive scrutiny. In Chapter Three, methods in individual music therapy are set out and, in Chapter Four, the methods which are used in group music therapy.

Care Through the Medium of Music-Making

In this chapter general theoretical characteristics of care through the medium of music-making are explored. First of all, we will pause to deal with aspects of method in general: what difference does it make that 'doing something musical' is a form of care rather than a music lesson, for example? Following this, a breakdown is made of the different forms of care, in which music is used. In this chapter the distinction is made between musical activities, remedial music-making and music therapy. In the first section of the chapter, in which the general characteristics of care are discussed, the term 'music therapy' is used as a generic concept. However, when references are later made to music therapy in its narrower sense, this term is then only used in its specific meaning.

Care is a consciously-planned activity

Even though music is used by many who are employed in caring for people with developmental disabilities, it is not, however, true to say that all these people are practising music therapy. Learning to play an instrument at a music school, for instance, is not a form of music therapy, no more than is listening to a record with a friend. However, playing a musical instrument under the guidance of a music therapist may well constitute a form of music therapy, in the same way as listening to a record selected by the music therapist. In short, it obviously does not depend on the music itself as to whether a musical activity is called 'music therapy' or not, but rather on the intention of how the music is to be used in a specific situation. In this chapter we will discuss exactly what music therapy entails: a consciously planned form of care through the medium of music.

The fact that music therapy is a consciously planned activity means that it is the methodical use of music which is involved rather than making music 'willy-nilly'. Working methodically requires the music therapist to produce a plan of his activities in the light of a number of general principles. Therefore, irrespective of what the working environment of the therapist is like and of how the care is organised there, the music therapist will always have to give an explanation of the following points for consideration.

Care is offered for clear reasons

First, the music therapist should ask himself what the reasons are for offering his client a form of treatment and, if he is to do so, whether caring through music really is the most appropriate form of care for the person concerned. Questions such as, for which complaints treatment is appropriate, which form of care is then most suitable and which method of working (individual or in a group) should be used, point to the need for indications to be given. Examples of such indications for music therapy might include things such as: the client avoiding contact with others; his failure to come into his own in his community; the existence of obvious emotional problems; and so forth. Why he should now specifically be offered music therapy and not any other form of care, is often an intuitive decision. Hardly any fixed rules exist about this and so the experience of the therapist has a large role to play in this decision.

Besides there being good reason for offering somebody music therapy, there may also be grounds for actually refraining from offering it. These so-called contra-indications are partly based on the attitude of the client as regards music. For example, if a client is so firmly attached to one particular musical skill that everything that the music therapist offers is rejected, music therapy would be contra-indicated. Sometimes all the client wants to do is to play his own, familiar tunes on the penny whistle, in the same way as he has already been proudly playing them to others for years on end. The non-musical behaviour of the client can also be a reason for not offering music therapy; for example, when he has such kinds of stereotypical movements that contact with the music therapist is impeded. However, the preference of the therapist himself also has a large role to play; what one music therapist might consider a contra-indication, another can actually see as a challenge to continue to look for a musical approach.

It is preferable and, in fact, necessary for the music therapist not to make a decision about the suitability of the client for music therapy by himself, but for the team working in the institution to think it through and to come to a joint decision about it. In a small institution, such as a child day care centre or an adult day care centre, this team will commonly consist of any 'experts' who are present, as well as the group leaders. In a larger institution such as a residential institution, a referral for music therapy will often come from the team working on the client's ward. A (contra-)indication is then specified in consultation with the team working on the ward to which music therapy is attached (for example activity therapy, or the educational psychology department). The weighing up of the indications and contra-indications is an important factor in the methodical use of music. In the following chapter, in which different methods are discussed, it will become clear that making a careful judgement about a client's suitability will also give direction to the objective which is to be pursued in the course of the therapy. With this in mind, we arrive at the following consideration: setting the objective of care.

Care is appropriated in the light of the objectives

An important part of working methodically is that the therapist consciously pursues specific objectives. If he knows that a certain client will be coming to him for treatment, he needs to establish which objectives are to be pursued for the client and with the client.

Sometimes it is possible for the therapist to talk through and set these objectives with the client. Referral for music therapy will then become easier for the client to understand; he has a say in the choice of treatment and is able to be aware of what it entails. In practice, conferring will not always be possible. The therapist and his team interpret the client's needs and assume that it is in the best interests of the client to pursue a certain objective.

By setting concrete objectives, the therapist can establish how to go about assisting the client. In practice, many objectives are feasible. Examples of objectives include the therapist working at building channels of communication with the client to resolve psychological problems or to stimulate motor skills. Emphasis can also be placed on experiencing pleasure in making music and the goal of developing or strengthening self-confidence.

In order to be able to evaluate whether the objective can be attained and where the best starting-points appear to be, the therapist is able to gather information about the client before treatment begins. However, some music therapists are of the opinion that it is better to know as little as possible about the client before treatment begins. It is preferable for them not to read any reports beforehand and it frequently occurs that they do choose not to gather any information. The idea behind this way of working is that a client will benefit the most if the therapist can approach him with an open mind.

There are some disadvantages attached to this point of view. People with a developmental disability who have lived in an institution throughout their lives, have dealings with an awful lot of care workers, who often follow on from one another in rapid succession. Again and again the demand is made of the person with a developmental disability to adapt to new care workers and to embark on yet another fresh relationship. Regrettably, it is seldom the case that he can experience a living environment, free from disruption, as far as people are concerned. The necessary continuity in care can be guaranteed, at least to some extent, if the care worker is prepared to find out what the experiences of other care workers have been. Of course the client has a right to have the therapist approach him as openly as possible, but he has just as much a right to respect earned from his earlier experiences with care workers, experiences which he himself will often only be able to articulate with great difficulty. Moreover, it is a misnomer to suppose that forming a personal opinion on the basis of collected information equates to being prejudiced.

In practice, the music therapist will first of all collect the information which is available within the institution. This can mean reading files, but may also involve also visiting the client in his community and talking with the staff. He might even contact the parents to determine whether, for example, the client has any experience of music, and if so what kind of experiences these were. By giving himself plenty of time to gather the information, the therapist can form a basis for beginning the treatment.

Sometimes the therapist needs a number of sessions to set his objective. With time, he can turn the objective, which was set by the team, into an objective specific to music therapy. What is more, during the sessions, intermediate objectives can be set, in which it is made clear by what intermediate steps the objective can ultimately be attained. This preparatory stage in the treatment can determine the accuracy of the assessment for music therapy, but can sometimes lead to a premature conclusion of the treatment. The latter can occur when, during the first session, contra-indications become apparent which had not been foreseen.

The choice of techniques is to be planned beforehand

When the music therapist and the client finally take the plunge together, the assessment of the client's suitability for music therapy is made and confirmed, the information is collected and his long-term and short-term objectives are set. It is at this juncture that the therapist will have to decide with the help of which techniques he will endeavour to attain his objectives. The relationship between the pursued objectives and the techniques employed is not always straightforward in practice. The choice of techniques is, in part at least, dependent upon the client: which instruments are preferable for him? Which techniques are suitable or not suitable for his level of functioning? Furthermore, as will be seen in the following chapter, some techniques are more appropriate than others in attaining a particular objective. What also has to be taken into consideration is that choosing certain techniques and musical instruments is partly determined by the experience and personal preferences of the therapist.

In the course of the treatment, not only can the objectives be adjusted but the techniques can also be changed. The fact that these changes are made during the therapy process should speak for itself.

For virtually every client, music therapy is a process which comes to an end after a certain time; namely, when the objectives have been attained. This point of view is not shared by all music therapists. Some suggest that music therapy with people with developmental disabilities is essentially open-ended; music therapy is, to their mind, a life-long learning process. The methods which are described in this book are based on the first of these points of view. Even though the person with a developmental disability is in constant need of care, the objectives of the care through music therapy are set such that it is possible to realize them eventually, thus obviating the need for specialist help. Should a new need become apparent after attaining the objective, then what form of care is the most appropriate has to be evaluated again.

Particularly when working with people with severe developmental disabilities, it seems impossible that the treatment will ever come to an end; indeed they will for ever be dependent on extensive help. However, even if this is the case, the music therapist should still set his objectives realistically. The objective may be, for example, to draw the client out of his own little world and to face him with the outside world. If, after a number of years of therapy, this has (to some extent) been achieved, consideration must be given anew as to whether music therapy is still desirable. It may be that the place of the music therapist is replaced by an activity supervisor or by the group leaders, or it may even be decided (temporarily) to offer another form of specialist help or to suspend therapy altogether. It is likewise conceivable that new objectives are set and that the music therapist continues to work with the client.

In order to remain in touch during the course of the music therapy, the team must be kept informed at regular intervals. Concluding the treatment should also, ideally, take place in consultation with the team.

To summarise, the music therapist keeps the following things in mind:

- collecting biographical details
- collecting diagnostic information
- reasons for registering the client
- weighing up the choice of the form of care
- weighing up the option of not offering a certain form of care
- (temporary) setting ultimate and intermediate objectives
- (temporary) choice of techniques and instruments.

Thus far we have discussed general methodical characteristics to do with methods of music-making as a form of care.

The impression that all consciously planned activities should be along the same lines as music therapy may have been given. In the introduction to this chapter, however, it was noted that this is not the case. In practice, the term music therapy is actually used for very different forms of care, all based upon the fact that music takes a central position. In the following three sections we make the distinction between musical activities, remedial music-making and music therapy. We will discuss these three forms of care in more detail, in the course of which making the evaluation, setting the objective and choosing the techniques will once again be brought up for consideration.

What do we mean by musical activities?

Group leaders or care workers of people with developmental disabilities often hear from parents that their child gains a lot of pleasure from music; as a small child he literally followed the music, he swayed along to the beat of the music which was coming out of the radio and now that he is a little older, as soon as he gets home, he switches on the record player in his room. Although some music therapists, as well as other experts, are of the opinion that people with developmental disabilities, and particularly those with Down syndrome, are very musical rhythmically, even more musical than the non-developmentally disabled, others suggest that this is not true. They think that the ability to hear and, thus, the ability to listen to music, is often one of the faculties which has not been affected by the developmental disability. Thus there is no more or less musical aptitude displayed in those with a developmental disability than in those without a developmental disability. One possible explanation of this is that the processing of rhythm is localised in the lower parts of the brain, parts which are often less affected by the disability. However, because their appreciation of music is relatively unaffected, music can be extremely significant in their lives.

Music-making can be an important way of spending one's free time for a person with a developmental disability. In many institutions, more often than not, music is made for or by the residents in their community. Sometimes these activities take the form of a music lesson and the music therapist is (also) attached to the institution's school. If this is the case, then they do not talk about musical activities but about music education. This is particularly evident in special education and less so in institutions and child day care centres. In this book we do not aim to look at music education but rather to give consideration to musical activities. This includes different ways of making music together, ways which might be encouraged without any intention of giving a music lesson. Examples of musical activities include singing in a choir, playing in an orchestra or in a drum band or preparing to put on a musical. Musical activities are characterised by the following three aspects:

1. Education and development by means of and in music.
2. The activity takes a central place.
3. No specific responsibility for the music therapist.

1. Education and development in and through music

The first characteristic of musical activities is that the therapist's starting point is education and development in and through music. To do this, the client is familiarized with the music and its many modes of expression. There is a broad spectrum of interpretations for the term music; it can refer to instrumental music, but also to sound from one's natural environment, in which aspects such as rhythm, volume, how sound is experienced, and the like, are important. One of the most important objectives in musical activities is that the client derives a sense of pleasure from making music and through doing so has the chance to develop self-confidence. As well as this, 'knowing about music' can constitute an objective, whilst learning to play a musical instrument or learning to sing can be pursued as secondary objectives. In this respect, musical activities are like activities in music education, as we know them in the form of general music training.

2. The activity takes a central place

As the therapist weighs up which methods to apply, the musical activity plays a more a central role than the personality of the client. Of course, that is not to say that the client is not important! All that is meant by this is that the most important starting point for the therapist is the musical activity. Thus, the therapist can first decide to set up a drum band and then follow this by looking for potential members for it. The techniques are set out from the beginning; the therapist opts for one particular repertoire, decides which instruments he wishes to use and shares them out amongst the clients (with or without consultation of the client's wishes). Subsequently, arriving at a musical end product takes precedence in the musical activity; playing well together, a flawless performance of a musical, putting on a Nativity play, and so forth. How the individual client fits into this is the therapist's second point, although very important, for consideration.

3. No specific responsibility for the music therapist

This final characteristic implies that, for the supervision of a musical activity, the specific expertise of the music therapist is not required, as will become clear after reading the explanation of the two other types of care through music. Since, with musical activities, it is not a question of the music therapist supervising a process which the client is undergoing, his specific expertise is therefore not a prerequisite for being able to supervise musical activities. It is even a moot point as to whether a music therapist should have to take on these kinds of activities in his range of responsibilities; a supervisor of musical activities or a musician is able to direct the musical goings-on just as expertly. It may be that the specific expertise of a music therapist can be put into action in a supervisory capacity in watching over the activity supervisors or the musicians. The music therapist is, after all, jointly responsible for the use of music in his institution. On this point, Adriaansz and Stijlen (1986) make reference to advising and supervising in looking at the sound environment, the acquisition and use of musical toys, instruments and musical apparatus or the installation of rooms for 'hug therapy'.

What do these three aspects now mean in the context of the methodical use of musical activities?

It is clear that, on the whole, there will be no indication for musical activities. Anyone who wishes and is able to take part in the activity is actually 'indicated'. Notice can, for example, be given by means of the institution's newspaper, an announcement made by the group leaders or by the music therapist who may himself be sounding out possible participants. The way in which the activity is offered is always in a group situation.

In practice it might, obviously, come about that a certain client does not appear suitable to participate in any musical activities. Directly observable behaviour on the past of the client can in particular provide a good reason for making a contra-indication. If his musical or non-musical behaviour is disruptive in such a way that the musical end product is hindered as a result, this can constitute a reason for not allowing the client to take part in the activities. In such a case the therapist can assess whether offering an individual activity is a viable alternative.

Even though no specific individual objectives are set for musical activities on the whole, the activities can still be of great significance to the client. Participation in a musical activity can provide him with a great sense of pleasure and could even contribute to the development or strengthening of his self-confidence. For others, participation in a music group can lead on, amongst other things, to becoming accustomed to order and learning to adapt to arrangements and rules. Virtually every music therapist who writes on this subject is of the opinion that participation in musical activities can be of great value for a person with a developmental disability.

As for the choice of technique, as I have already pointed out, this is mostly done beforehand by the music therapist. The client actually applies for certain activities such as playing with others, singing, putting on a musical, and so forth. The chosen products are mostly geared towards seeing an end product; it is self-evident that an audible musical result is indeed sought after.

What do we mean by remedial music-making?

The term 'remedial music-making'

The term 'remedial' (from the Latin *remediare*, meaning 'to make better') is, for example, used in care in connection with words such as remedial education and remedial teaching. What these 'types of care' have in common is that they are extended to people whose development, either physical or mental, has been disrupted. For their education, teaching and care, specific methodologies have been developed to stimulate the disrupted or arrested development.

It is also used in the sense of extending care to people with socio-emotional problems and catering for their further development (van Beugen 1986). Such types of care are necessary when the living environment and surroundings, in certain respects, are unable to cater for this kind of development. This is often the case in caring for people with developmental disabilities. In the normal context of home, for many reasons insufficient opportunities are available (in the long run) to look after the child and stimulate him in his development. Professional, remedial care is then called for. But even when the client's developmental progress is complete, some form of care usually remains a necessity for people with developmental disabilities in order to stabilise or improve the client's ability to function in his living environment.

Remedial action has three characteristics:

1. It is worked at methodically; beforehand a plan is made, which is subsequently carried out and evaluated.

2. Through consultation, a relationship of professional cooperation between therapist and client(s) is initiated.

3. Working to a plan and initiating the relationship of cooperation can be aimed at bringing about changes in the psychological and social structures in which the client is living, as well as at improving his ability to function.

It is essential that the pursued objectives fall within the values and standards which the client himself espouses. If we are working with people with developmental disabilities, a potential problem poses itself at this point. The standards and values espoused by the person with a developmental disability often have to be interpreted by the care worker and are often more a reflection of the standards and values of the living environment of the non-developmentally disabled. The care worker will consequently have to police himself more critically on this point. In any case, the interpreted standards and values must not conflict with those of the society to which the client and therapist belong.

Now that the term 'remedial' has been explained, what remedial music-making means should become self-evident. It is possible to place extremely divergent emphases on remedial action. For example, sometimes the therapist endeavours to modify the psychological and social structures in which the client is living. He is then able to help the client to make himself more competent by offering him group treatment or by helping him to develop communication skills. Examples of other emphases are, to name a few, the development of motor skills, the improvement of concentration, or the stimulation of individual expression.

In caring for people with developmental disabilities, it is of the utmost importance that the different types of care within an institution are geared towards one another. The different forms of treatment are not to be offered in isolation; an atmosphere must be created in which change and development are possible. What is more, remedial music-making must be incorporated in this, if it is to have any effect at all. Participation in team discussions and a formal system of communicating the music therapist's experiences are necessary prerequisites. The distance created between care from experts and care from the group does not need to be any greater than is structurally necessary. This does not mean, however, that remedial music-making always has to take place within or with the group with which the client lives. In the following chapters we will see that a starting point of this kind militates against correct prescription and reduces the chance of working purposefully.

It has probably already become clear to the reader who is well read in the literature on music therapy that large parts of the methods which, in practice, are referred to as music therapy, are, in fact, to be looked upon as types of remedial music-making. Publications by pioneers such as Alvin, Nordoff and Robbins or Lecourt also largely describe remedial work with people with developmental disabilities.

It has to be noted that some people talk about music-making in remedial education rather than remedial music-making. This distinction is, in part, related to different ways of looking at developmental disabilities. From one point of view, if we believe that a person with a developmental disability will never attain the functional age of an adult, then we believe that it is still possible to carry on looking upon him as a 'child'; if that is the case, care can be seen as a continuous process of education, which is covered by the term 'remedial education'. Another basic assumption might be that the person with a developmental disability has 'blossomed' within his own range of capabilities. At this point the educator must stop and the transition should be made to remedial action, as care is still necessary.

Another interpretation of remedial action, as opposed to remedial education, is set out by Adriaansz and Stijlen (1986). They make the distinction between music therapy as a psychotherapy and music therapy as used in remedial education. In the case of the latter, the music therapist should be geared towards developing the individual faculties of the person with a developmental disability. His objectives might then, for example, be: learning to talk; learning to concentrate; developing self-awareness. Music therapy, characteristic of a remedial education, commonly takes place in groups and is geared towards learning to work together, live together and play together.

Indications for remedial music-making

Now that the field of remedial music-making has been outlined, we can show how it fits in with methodology.

Making a diagnosis of a client's suitability generally takes place on the basis of quite broadly-based judgments: it may be suspected, for example, that the client still has the capacity for growth, that he is opting out of the group, or that the members of a group are not really experiencing much of a sense of community. Such indications describe the client in terms of growth, development or his ability to function in the group. What the break-down of the client's personality is like and whether psychological problems are at hand, hardly plays a part in this kind of judgment, if at all. It also happens that no specific recommendation for music-making is made, for instance because it is thought that 'making music benefits everyone', because the client loves music, or because music-making is set out according to a detailed schedule. In the last case, the referral for music-making is consequently based more or less on chance circumstances.

In practice, there are hardly any reasons for not offering remedial music-making. Contra-indications play a very subordinate role as regards method.

Objectives of remedial music-making

In remedial music-making it is, in fact, necessary to distinguish clearly between objectives and the working methods used in musical activities. The groups of objectives include:

- stimulating individual growth
- developing and stimulating social skills
- developing and stimulating cognitive skills
- developing and stimulating motor skills.

The creation of opportunities for personal growth is an extremely important objective in remedial music-making. The concept of growth in this context is closely related to the point of view that the moments in which the person experiences himself as being 'whole' can contribute to self-realization. By making music, or by listening to it, the client is offered enriching experiences, which can also be seen as feelings of self-realization. In achieving this, the music therapist makes use of specific qualities in music: sensitivity, great accessibility, structural protection and absence of the spoken word. In practice, the pursuit of these relatively vague, but still very important, concepts is referred to in different ways. Ter Burg (1986) talks, for example, about 'music-making as a vehicle for opening oneself up, realizing one's full potential and for development'. Others set objectives such as 'in making music, the client can experience security and discover new opportunities for individual expression' or 'music-making can be a positive experience which can lead to self-consolidation'.

The second group of objectives, the stimulation of social skills, is generally pursued by offering group treatment. A wide range of objectives can exist: learning to observe oneself and others; working at socialization; learning to communicate with one's circle of acquaintances, and so forth. In the concrete action taken by the therapist, the difference can once again be seen between musical activities and remedial music-making. With musical activities, decisions about which technique to use are mostly made on the basis of musical determinants. In remedial music-making, however, the decisions about the musical techniques are principally governed by factors concerning the client's social welfare. If the therapist has to choose how much further to go during the session, in deciding what to do, he will attach more importance to the interactional scope of the technique than to the technicalities of the music. This can, on certain occasions, cause problems, as music is then relegated to the role of being merely a tool and its essential quality is distorted. If this is the case, the music therapist will have to decide upon one method, in which 'justice is done' to both the interactional and musical considerations.

There is more to be observed about the stimulation of social skills, notably that social skills which can be stimulated are, more than any, based on the abilities of the client himself. The therapist endeavours to develop every individual form of expression, so that interaction can result between unique individuals. This endeavour will often fail to tally on the one hand with teaching or coaching in social skills, which relate fundamentally to the value system of the non-developmentally disabled, and on the other with teaching certain social conventions. Furthermore, in applying these objectives in practice, emphasis is placed on learning to deal with each person's individual way of being. In other words, the music therapist attempts to smooth off the rough edges of socially inappropriate behaviour and to offer new behavioural options. At the same time he devotes particular attention to developing the skills of his clients, in order to establish points of contact, which come about as a result of mutual acceptance. In discussing (individual) music therapy, a description will be given of the shift of emphasis onto problems induced intra-psychologically, in relating to other people. The music therapist will, in this case, endeavour to resolve or minimize the problems which are connected with socially inappropriate behaviour or withdrawn behaviour, in order to achieve the essential change, in the way contact with others is made.

The third group of objectives which can be pursued in remedial music-making is the development and stimulation of cognitive skills. As with musical activities, the music therapist is attempting to teach the client 'something'. Whilst teaching about music and deriving pleasure from making music are indeed central to musical activities, with remedial music-making it is exclusively learning through music which remains of central importance in pursuing this objective: getting involved in music might be looked upon as the trimmings of teaching. Some music therapists are themselves of the opinion that this area of cognitive growth is the most important area of all those in which they wish to get involved. However, this results in an (over) restricted use of the opportunities which working with music has to offer.

In practice, a whole range of objectives are set in which the stimulation of cognitive skills plays a central role. It might, for example, be important to work on increasing the concentration span of the client, as this may be the prerequisite for the client to be able to give structure to the things influencing him in his environment. Moreover, a longer concentration span simplifies the process of learning from experience. By extension, the objective is that the client learns to correct himself through music-making, so as to correct himself when performing non-musical tasks. There are still many other types of cognitive objectives possible; for instance, in the area of language development.

The final group of objectives is geared towards stimulating the motor skills. Although movement therapy and psychomotor therapy are also available for people with developmental disabilities, in most institutions the stimulation of motor skills can constitute a considerable proportion of the music therapist's work. On the one hand, the therapist can pursue objectives which affect the whole body, such as developing physical consciousness, learning to use the five senses or stimulating eye-hand coordination. On the other hand, he can also set objectives which affect the stimulation of specific bodily functions, such as breathing, speech development or fine motor control.

Techniques for remedial music-making

Given this description of the indications and the objectives for remedial music-making, we will very briefly outline which techniques are generally used. Similarly, there are specific characteristics of remedial music-making as regards the therapist–client relationship and the use of musical tools (and possibly also movement tools).

First and foremost, it is extremely important that the therapist creates a safe atmosphere and builds up a good working relationship with the client. As in the case of music therapy, the therapist working in remedial music-making takes, for the most part, a fundamentally Rogerian (client-centred) approach and, where necessary, complements this with a more direct approach. This means that he will attempt to accept the client as much as possible in whatever way he may present himself, so that he can put himself in the place of the client (empathy), and so that he can endeavour as much as possible to be himself (integrity). The latter of these is especially important in caring for people with developmental disabilities, as coping with the differences in the levels of development between the care worker and the client can be a pitfall. An approach which is too childish ('come on, little one...') or which is too familiar ('are you playing then, guys...?') does not really do justice to the integrity of the client. Even though he is, of course, to be met on his own level (and the therapist adapts himself to this level), the therapist's basic attitude in this respect does not differ from his attitude in working with the non-developmentally disabled. By fulfilling these conditions for therapy and by offering a structured opportunity for treatment, an atmosphere can be created in which it is safe for the client to learn, to develop himself, or to change.

The difference, however, with music therapy is that the therapeutic relationship is never, or hardly ever, methodically conducted. After all, the idea behind remedial music-making is primarily that the objectives are attained by using musical tools. Bringing about a change, by methodically working at a client–therapist relationship as well as the client's relationship to the music, is of central importance, above all in music therapy.

We may therefore conclude that in remedial music-making it is a matter of how to handle musical tools. Learning to carry out musical activities and arriving at a final product is of secondary importance compared to developing and stimulating both a range of skills and personal growth. The emphasis lies far less on completing a process intended to resolve individual psychological problems than is the case with music therapy. In remedial music-making, what is important is that the use of musical tools provides the client with a pleasurable activity, thus enabling him to be stimulated. The way in which the tools are given to the client is generally set out beforehand and planned on the basis of the remedial objective.

What do we mean by music therapy?

The third type of care through music-making is music therapy. This type of care is, in theory, clearly distinguishable from the working methods of musical activities and remedial music-making. In practice, it is possible for music therapy to be integrated with remedial music-making. This appears especially to be the case with individual treatment and hardly at all with group treatment. Music therapy is never concerned with the level of musical activities: in practice, they are mutually exclusive.

Looking at the term 'music therapy' in more detail

In this section I shall demonstrate how music therapy can be a form of psychotherapeutic care for people with developmental disabilities. As, however, music therapy has become an accepted term in everyday language, and is used to refer to musical activities and remedial music-making as well as to music therapy, in the book, *Grondslagen van Muziektherapie* (Schalkwijk 1984) it was suggested that the term 'music psychotherapy' should be introduced. As a result, it was possible to use the word 'music therapy' as a generic term, in which the term 'therapy' is used in the same way as it is in the terms physiotherapy, drug therapy or occupational therapy. Thus, it ought to be possible to nominate music psychotherapy as a working method, in which action is firmly rooted in the methodology of psychotherapy.

Since 1984, the year in which *Grondslagen van muziektherapie* (Schalkwijk) was published, there have been various developments, as a result of which the use of the term music psychotherapy is still not yet being used accurately. This is mainly connected with the fact that there has been much debate in music therapy and pressure for a professional register of music therapists to be set up, while at the same time the term 'remedial (educational) music-making' has also found a separate place in individual training colleges. Because of this, a (theoretical) distinction ought to be made between music therapy, remedial music-making and musical activities. This obviates the need to introduce the term 'music psychotherapy'. Nevertheless, as is noted in Chapter Five, in daily practice a music therapist uses both music therapy and remedial music-making and fulfils a supervisory/advisory role on the subject of musical activities.

The basic principle of this book is, in any case, that music therapy should be regarded as a type of psychotherapy for people with developmental disabilities. The characteristics of psychotherapy, as applied to music therapy, have been scarcely touched upon in the literature to date, forcing us to seek information from the theory of verbal psychotherapy, in order to understand this subject. There are many definitions of psychotherapy, but broadly speaking there is unanimity over the following point. In psychotherapy, the distinction is made between three dimensions: there is the client, there is the psychotherapist and there is the process of psychotherapy. Not everyone can work using psychotherapy. To be able to carry out methodical treatment, you must have completed some kind of specialist training. Psychotherapy treatment is offered to clients who need help with psychological difficulties, conflicts or disorders.

The therapist is endeavouring to establish methodically, give structure to and handle a relationship with the aim of resolving or minimizing the psychological difficulties, conflicts or disorders. One important supposition in music therapy is that the client's psychological problems will indeed manifest themselves as the music therapist and the client make music together. As the therapist is highly sensitive to such manifestations, he can attempt to get the problems 'out in the open' using the medium of music. The problems are subsequently worked through during the process of music-making, by experiencing them in different ways in the therapy. For this process, the ways of using the musical tools and the handling of the therapeutic relationship by the therapist are, amongst others, important methods of approach.

Evidently, differences are detectable between remedial music-making and musical activities on the one hand, and music therapy on the other. In the first two of these categories, the therapist's character and the handling of the therapeutic relationship play a relatively small role as regards method, if any (although with remedial music-making, sometimes an affective process comes into play). This, then, affects the process of change in a way similar to that which the client might experience in music therapy. In Chapter Three the therapy process and how the therapeutic relationship is handled is explored in more detail.

One other difference between music therapy, and musical activities in particular, has to do with the skills and the knowledge that the music therapist is deemed to have.

Besides having a knowledge of music and a traditional command of music, the music therapist also has insight into how to handle methodically a therapeutic relationship. To be able to assess which methods are the most suitable for a client, it is recommended that the therapist oversees the possible options for and restrictions of treatment in the different types of care. This puts him in a position of being able to tailor his choice of a certain method of music therapy to the specific problem area of the client. For treating compulsive behaviour, he can, for example, opt for a more direct approach, such that the client is closely supervised within a rigid framework. For treating an identity crisis, by contrast, a Rogerian attitude is a more appropriate method. Consequently, the therapist chooses a frame of reference for his course of actions, which is dependent on evaluating which is the most appropriate form of care.

The impression may have been given from the above that the music therapist for the most part (or even exclusively) gears himself towards types of verbal psychotherapy. There is, however, nothing further from the truth than this. While knowledge of verbal psychotherapy gives the music therapist insight into some general factors in psychotherapy, ideally, the music therapist should be informed about the specific workings of other types of creative therapy. It is important that he knows about both movement and movement therapy, as well as other non-verbal methods. Furthermore, the music therapist should be in a position to be able to use his own emotional sensitivity and his own verbal and non-verbal modes of expression within the therapeutic relationship. To be able to work with your own emotions and with those of a client, at the very least, an individual learning therapy is to be recommended, preferably a form of music therapy, so that work can be carried out with insight.

Finally, it is also important that the music therapist feels at home with developmental psychology, psychopathology and the study of neuroses. This knowledge is, after all, necessary to be able to work with people with developmental disabilities, who are suffering from psychological conflicts and disorders.

Methodical characteristics of music therapy

If we study the methodical elements of music therapy, such as indications, objectives and techniques, we may note the following things.

One thing that music therapy has in common with remedial music-making is that it is essential that the client is assessed as suitable for treatment by this method. The nature of the indication is, however, quite different. With remedial music-making, the indications are mainly based on resolving problems which are primary or secondary in their effect on the developmental (or physical) disability. With music therapy, the indications are based on psychological difficulties, conflicts or disorders, which can exist alongside the effects of the developmental disability. In saying this I am not, however, claiming that there is not an interplay between each of the areas of indication. In this way more recognition is given to the fact that people with developmental disabilities, as a result of their disability, are actually extremely vulnerable to psychological conflicts and disorders.

If we look more closely at the nature of the objectives which are pursued in music therapy, the difference between remedial music-making and music therapy becomes clearer.

With remedial music-making, general objectives can easily be set, which may apply for several clients. With music therapy this is less viable, as the causes of the psychological conflicts or disorders, and the way in which they manifest themselves, can actually differ greatly. The objectives will in this case usually be formulated in terms of resolving the disorder or working through the conflict. Possible examples of concrete objectives are: working through the death of the parents; drawing the client out of his own little world and facing him with the outside world; minimizing feelings of guilt regarding one's perception of sexuality and one's sexual identity. Building up a relationship between client and therapist can, in the early stages, be an explicit objective in music therapy.

The concrete techniques which are used in music therapy do not generally differ greatly from the techniques which, for example, are employed in remedial music-making. There are three characteristics of techniques used in music therapy.

One essential component of music therapy is handling a therapeutic relationship in the treatment of psychological difficulties, conflicts or disorders. To do this, two remedies are available to the therapist: the client's use of the musical tools, and the music therapist–client relationship. Of course, in working with people with developmental disabilities, discussing the therapist–client relationship is seldom one of the options open in handling the relationship. For this reason, the therapist will handle the client–music relationship as well as the client–therapist relationship mainly by using musical techniques (this is explored in more detail in Chapter Three). It must also be observed that, in principle, the same applies for music therapy for the non-developmentally disabled. In this instance too, the methodical use of relationships is mainly used through the client's use of the musical tools. This does not detract from the fact that even talking can play a part in music therapy.

The second characteristic is that, in music therapy, going through a therapeutic process is of primary importance. The choice of techniques is also determined by what attempts are made at getting the process going. In contrast to remedial music-making, techniques are consequently formulated which dictate how the therapeutic relationship is handled. As an example, let us cite the techniques where the therapist varies the level of his activities and, by doing so, breaks through some of the client's expectations.

The third characteristic, finally, is that the use of musical tools is significantly different from that in remedial music-making and musical activities. The process of therapy is primary, and arriving at a musical product is secondary to the necessity of letting the process run its course. The planning, completion and evaluation of the techniques employed are done mainly on the basis of the objectives, whereas with musical activities (and to a lesser degree with remedial music-making) these are done from the point of view of what musical product is desired. Generally speaking, it is possible to ascertain that the more the therapist's work is geared towards a process, the less important established activities become, whereas musical improvisation is, on the other hand, going to play an increasingly large role.

Conclusion

The difference between the three forms of care, which we have discussed here, can be illustrated with an example, in which the differences are over-accentuated a little. With musical activities, learning to play an electric organ can be made possible with the help of a colour notation system. The therapist will practise with the client just long enough for him to hear the chosen tune. If it still seems too difficult, he will urge him to carry on with it and possibly to practise the tune in smaller sections. Even with remedial music-making, learning to play a musical instrument can be set as an objective. The therapist endeavours to structure the learning in such a way that the client is frustrated as little as possible. For example, what might be of major importance to him is that, time and again, the client finds that he can actually do something. Whether there will ever be a tune to listen to, is of secondary importance, as long as the client considers playing to be something positive. In music therapy, the therapist will try and avoid the idea that a 'feat of learning' must be achieved. He should usually put the idea of learning to play an instrument to one side and instead should improvise. In doing so there is more of a chance that the client will discover what he can do and what his limits and problems are in using musical tools.

In this chapter, three forms of working with music have been described: musical activities, remedial music-making and music therapy. In the following two chapters, methods are set out in which the different types of care are examined in more detail. From now on, the term music therapy is no longer used as a generic term, as was sometimes the case in Chapters One and Two. Whenever music therapy is now mentioned, the use of music as a psychotherapeutic method of care is the intended meaning.

The methods described in Chapters Three and Four are frameworks, within which each therapist can incorporate his own working method. The methods are possible blueprints for practical situations, but not an identical reproduction of the same practical situation. Whoever goes looking for 'the' form of care through the medium of music-making in the following chapters, will probably be disappointed. Every therapist can recognise and develop his own methods on the basis of the methods which are outlined.

CHAPTER 3

Individual Treatment

When should individual treatment be offered?

Opting for individual treatment is not always an easy choice to justify. Sometimes it appears mainly to be the intuition of the music therapist, or of the other team members, which determines that an individual approach appears more suitable than a group approach. Yet there are also concrete considerations which should lead to opting for individual therapy.

It is usually the case that the more serious the problems of the client are, the more obvious this choice will be. It can be observed of people with developmental disabilities that their capacity for integrating external influences with their own impulses is, on the whole, poorly developed, or hardly developed at all. In other words, it is a question of a deficient ego-function. Everyday functioning involves the fact that, if there are emotional problems, the person with the developmental disability will only be able to accept this with some difficulty. We must always be aware of the fact that there is a continual interplay between

- the emotional problems which result from an unsuccessful integration of impulses, desires and demands from the outside world and

- a limit to the capacity for integrating these elements which is necessary in order to overcome such emotional problems.

Environment also plays an important part in this: in interacting with others, the person with a developmental disability can endeavour to strengthen himself once again in such a way that he can overcome his problems. The more severe the client's problems are, such as psychotic disorders or strong aggressive urges, for example, the more the environment must have structure to it. A one-to-one, therapist-to-client situation allows more opportunity for giving structure to integration between the client and his environment than group treatment does. This can be an important reason for opting for an individual approach. Only when there is a sufficient amount of ego-strength should group treatment, if so desired, also contribute to solving the problems (as regards social skills, for example). In the case of a client having this kind of poor ego-function, so much so that a group approach has been ruled out, opting for an individual approach is partly a 'negative' easy way out: individual treatment is deemed appropriate because group treatment has been ruled out. One might mistakenly conclude from this that, in theory, working in a group should be the best choice, rather than working individually.

However, there are other reasons why an individual approach may in fact, be more suitable; namely, because of the specific method of this way of working. A very general indication is that the client is expressing needs for individual attention because the attention which can be given to him in his community is insufficient. Opting for music rather than other activities is, in such a case, more or less an arbitrary choice, often determined by the client's preference for music. It should still be possible to be able to opt for individual movement therapy, if there is a wish for individual attention to be given.

We make the distinction between two groups of indications for individual treatment.

Psychological problems

Just like anyone else, a person with a developmental disability may also have psychological problems. In the Netherlands, Dosen, amongst others, has pointed this out in his book *Psychische stoornissen bij zwakzinnige kinderen*. The way in which the disorder manifests itself is, in fact, sometimes different from the way in which it presents in the non-developmentally disabled; however, the root of the disorder is the same. People with a developmental disability, too, can have fears, conflicts or psychotic complaints because they have feelings which come into conflict. Dosen suggests that they run a higher risk of developing psychological disorders, partly because the ego-functions are often poorly developed, or hardly developed at all.

The following examples show which psychological problems are meant by this. First, there are psychological disorders – the relatively severe complaints which go hand-in-hand with the ego-functions being seriously affected. Here, one might think of psychotic complaints, strong disinhibitions, aggressive behaviour, autism, long-term depression, and so forth. However, there are also emotional problems which create a problem for the client, but which do not result in the ego-functions being affected. We are referring here to neurotic problems, such as compulsive behaviour, a depressive state of mind, evasion of personal contact, grief that has not been dealt with and an identity disorder, to mention a few. These kinds of neurotic problems and psychological disorders can constitute an indication for music therapy.

Communicative problems

Another reason for offering individual treatment is problems in communicating with others, as distinct from emotional problems or disorders. With this kind of problem, what lies at the root is the fact that the person with the developmental disability, if left to his own devices, experiences difficulty in relating to other people. This, for example, can be caused by poor self-awareness, but also by a negative self-image. In practice, these kind of causes can, for example, be articulated as follows: the client does not have enough opportunities for communicating, lacks a fighting spirit, suffers from a fear of failure, or from dominant feelings of inferiority. Sometimes, however, these sorts of problems actually constitute an indication for a group approach. The decision in favour of one or the other form of treatment is made partly on the basis of the assessment of the client's ego-strength. In order to establish contact with others, a reliable degree of ego-strength must be present, otherwise the client will look upon the group as being too threatening and will continue to withdraw from interacting with members of the group. Communicative problems, as distinct from emotional problems and disorders, generally constitute an indication for individual remedial music-making.

A final observation concerns communicative problems in which speech or language disorders predominate. In such cases, group treatment is usually offered.

In the next two sections, two methods are described: individual music therapy and individual remedial music-making. Although, in theory, these two methods are distinct from one another, in everyday practice there may be a degree of overlap. Certain aspects, which are described in one of the two methods (for example, phases in therapy), in practice have a role to play in both methods. The therapist can, for example, decide to employ elements of music therapy in remedial music-making, whilst there can sometimes be a place for aspects of a remedial approach with music therapy. This is not surprising if we realise that having communication problems with the outside world can be closely interwoven with the client's emotional problems or psychological disorders. It is then dependent upon the assessment of the client, as to which of the two methods should be chosen.

If the therapist suspects that the client's ego-strength is very low, working through the emotional problems could become too much of a strain for the client. He can decide to work, initially, at learning to cope with the challenging behaviour and mainly at ego-strengthening until the most current problems have been resolved. It is usually only then possible to work on the client's emotional conflicts, which are at the root of the problems. The therapist (and his team) can obviously choose to leave the emotional problems suppressed and to end the treatment. But if, in the course of time, problems re-emerge, working through the emotional problems (if it is possible) is definitely necessary.

Individual music therapy

Recommendation and diagnosis are to precede therapy

Klaasje, a 23-year-old woman who had been living in the institution for two years, was recommended for music therapy by the psychologist on her ward. Prior to her admission, she had lived with her mother at home and she used to visit a day care centre for adults. Up to this time she was somewhat shy, but was functioning in a balanced way, and held the day care centre for adults very close to her heart. In the report submitted as a result of the ward conference to which the music therapist was sent, various matters were brought up. First, it was apparent that her problems began after her parents had divorced. The aggressive behaviour which then came about became so severe that, within six months, admission into the institution appeared inevitable. Even on the ward, Klaasje was capable of being very aggressive as soon as things started to go against her. The group leaders and the other residents suffered greatly as a result of her outbursts, which were accompanied by the destruction of furniture, screaming and crying. A second observation from the team was that, during the periods in which she was not angry, she was usually withdrawn and had little contact with others. Music therapy was requested after structured supervision and medical support had brought about little change.

On the basis of the reported information concerning Klaasje, the music therapist decided to accept the referral: he suspected that working with music might possibly be a form of treatment in which both the aggression and the withdrawn behaviour could be tackled. In addition, his first impression was that an individual working method was more appropriate in this case than a group approach. Apart from her aggressive moods, this was the main reason why Klaasje appeared to have so few positive relationships with others. There was quite a chance that she might be ostracized from the group fairly quickly, as the group members could only see her aggressive way of establishing contact with them. The treatment started with individual diagnostic sessions, in which his impressions were tested out and on the grounds of which specific objectives in music therapy were set.

As we have already noted, individual music therapy is especially indicated for clients with emotional problems and disorders. It should be noted that in general it is preferable for the music therapist not to work exclusively on the basis of the information from the person making the referral. It is important for there to be a period of music therapy observation and it is also important for the diagnosis to be made by the music therapist himself. It is in actually using musical tools that things seen in the client are able to come out into the open, which previously remained hidden. Combining both sources of information (information from others and personal observations) can ultimately result in specific objectives being set which can be pursued through music therapy. It is advisable that (once again) this is done in consultation with a team composed from a range of disciplines. In practice, there are hardly any considerations which result in a decision actually not to offer individual music therapy. It is possible that, at some time in the future, the particulars of music therapy will become so clear that it will be possible to say unequivocally when it is not suitable as a form of treatment.

What are the opportunities available to the music therapist on the basis of which observations and diagnoses can be made? Other than the psychologist or the remedial educationalist, he hardly has any measuring instruments, if any at all, on the basis of which direct conclusions can be drawn about the problem for which the client has been referred for music therapy (an exception is given below on this point). With music therapy, there will always be an intuitive interpretation of the client's behaviour on the part of the therapist. To streamline the interpretation as much as possible in this phase of the therapy, the following points are of particular importance.

OBSERVATION

Observation means studying a client in a systematic way in a music therapy situation, in order to gather information about him. Concerning observation, Fockema-Andreae noted that the identity of music therapy must come to the forefront, that the setting must be a secure one, and that it must have an appealing character to it. Besides this, she recommends that a working method is used which is both active and receptive. Observation of the client ought to take place, as far as it is possible, in a context which is fairly constant for the therapist; that is to say, he must endeavour to find a procedure before interpreting the observation sessions, which can always be repeated. By doing so, it will be more feasible for the therapist to, amongst other things, compare clients, and so any tendency to start treatment at once, before it is certain that this particular course should be initiated, can be corrected. On the other hand, observation constitutes an essential part of the treatment. At this point, the relationship between therapist and client begins and the client himself usually has an affective experience at the first session.

An extensive observation sheet has been compiled by Boxill, in which various aspects of the client's ability to function have been noted. These include:

- biographical details, type of disability, medication, test information
- general characteristics such as observable behaviour, eye contact, nervous movements
- motor skills (general and fine motor control, coordination)
- communication (voice, speech, use of non-verbal communication)
- ability to function cognitively (aspects of observation, amongst other things)
- ability to function affectionately (temperament, facial expressions, emotional reactions)
- ability to function socially
- specific modes of behaviour in making music.

DIAGNOSIS

Whenever the therapist attempts to arrive at a statement about the specific problems of the client on the basis of his observations, we are talking about a diagnosis. He endeavours to specify his observations by using diagnostic measuring instruments. However, there are very few measuring instruments which are available to the music therapist. We will look at three more closely.

At Middelo (a training institute for creative therapy) the 'appeal list' has been developed, which gives the music therapist insight into the break-down and organisation of the client's emotional needs, and offers him an answer as to whether these are conflicting needs. This appeal list is comprehensively described by Grabau and Visser. The working method is as follows. In one particular way the therapist offers the client instruments and notes down on the list of questions how the client deals with the instruments. He then deduces from this which emotional needs make the instruments appealing and whether there are emotional conflicts as a result of these needs.

Another diagnostic instrument is the scales which Nordoff and Robbins have developed in order to trace the combined playing between therapist and client. This involves the therapist improvising on a piano and asking the client to accompany him on a drum. Following this, the therapist judges the client's playing in the light of the two scales. The first scale reflects the therapist–client relationship in the musical activity, whilst the second scale traces the degree of musical communication.

A third instrument has been developed by Rider. With the help of fifteen types of game, the level of a client's ability to function cognitively can be determined in a reliable way, according to Piaget's theory of developmental psychology.

Both the appeal list and Nordoff and Robbins' scales have not as yet been investigated in such a way that they might be considered as standardised measuring instruments. Really they are instruments which, when combined with the experience and intuition of the music therapist, can provide diagnostic statements.

Which objectives are to be pursued in individual music therapy?

It did not appear easy to get Klaasje to come for music therapy. Although the music therapist had got to know her at the café and she already knew his face from the music evening in the grounds, Klaasje was very reluctant to go along to the music therapy room. The first five sessions, in which the music therapist mainly let her try out different instruments and took part a little in interactive musical activities, provided him with a picture which in some respects differed greatly from the information given by Klaasje's ward. In the way that she used the musical tools, the need to be appreciated came to light, whilst at the same time a strong aversion to any contact with the music therapist was seen. Her anger, which had been present in such strength on the ward turned out, during the observation sessions, to be limited to the moment the session had to come to an end. Often Klaasje used to run out past the music therapist back to the ward quite enraged!

The music therapist concluded that Klaasje was having great difficulty in letting go. Both when leaving the ward to go for her music therapy, and when returning once more to the ward, there was panic, which was accompanied by anger. He wondered whether this was possibly connected to her mild brain damage, which Klaasje aggravated to switch from one situation to another. But it could also very well be tied up with the divorce of her parents: letting go always evokes the fear of being let down and anger at being abandoned. The feeling of being let down became even more concrete when she was moved into the institution: after 'losing' her father she was now losing her mother too. If the divorce really was critical to her problems, then the following question posed itself: why did she react so strongly to the divorce? The music therapist suspected that Klaasje was essentially a fairly anxious person, who borrowed her personal feelings from the people who were most important to her. When others dropped away (mother and father respectively), the threat of losing herself emerged.

The long-term objective for the therapy became working through the problems of attachment and separation/individuation in general, and more particularly dealing with the parents' divorce. The short-term objectives, along which lines the therapy was (it was hoped) going to run, were building up a relationship, increasing self-esteem, working through problems of letting go, and rounding off the therapy, one after another. When these objectives had been set, the music therapist ended the observation period and the therapy was actually started. It would have been ideal if the therapy could have taken place twice a week. However, his schedule only allowed for the chance of meeting Klaasje once a week for 45 minutes.

From the examples given, it seems that setting an objective for music therapy is mainly based on the therapist's interpretation of the client's underlying conflicts. It is also scarcely possible to be able to give examples of the objectives of music therapy which are applicable to several clients. The basic elements can, however, be put together. If music therapy is called for, then, when setting the objectives, the relationship is established between the client's complaints and what the causes of them are (the psychodynamics). In the case of Klaasje, the complaint of 'aggressive behaviour' was connected to the problems of separation/individuation, insecurity about identity, not being able to control feelings of anger, and the relationship between them. Another important factor is that the objectives are set realistically. The therapist must be reasonably able to expect that the objectives can be realised within the allotted time. In underlining the limited nature of care, a distinction is made between music therapy and remedial music-making. A person with a developmental disability is truly dependent on the care which is directed towards him and his psychosocial environment for a great part of his life.

OBJECTIVES DURING THE DIFFERENT PHASES OF THE THERAPY

Music therapy runs in phases, all of which require an equal amount of attention from the therapist. At the beginning of therapy the emphasis lies on building up a therapeutic relationship between therapist and client. They still have to become attuned to one another and the client must gain confidence in working with the therapist.

Only when these conditions have been fulfilled will the client be able to express himself emotionally. Realizing the objective of this first phase of therapy sometimes takes months. The objective in the following phase is working through the problems which caused the client to come for therapy. In discussing the techniques, we will see that the therapeutic relationship is pre-eminently the means for working through the psychological problems. The last phase of therapy consists of rounding things off. In this phase the therapist assesses whether the changes are taking root and how the therapy can be wound down without the client feeling abandoned. A thorough rounding-off of events is extremely important, particularly for people with developmental disabilities, to prevent the client feeling once again let down by a care worker. It will probably occur seldom, if ever, in his life that he is the one who can choose to leave somebody else! As a rule it is usually appropriate that the winding-down phase lasts just as long as the building-up phase. All in all, a course of individual music therapy can last two years or longer.

PROCESS-ORIENTED OBJECTIVES ARE OF PRIME IMPORTANCE

As regards the nature of the objectives, it can be generally noted that process-oriented work is infinitely preferable to product-oriented work. This implies that the therapist should avoid aiming to give musical instruction or to encourage musical development. This would only call for a strong product orientation from both client and therapist. By constantly bearing in mind during therapy that emotional problems are resolved by going through a process, the therapist can gear his actions to controlling this process. This sometimes means that the therapy runs an erratic course: the client regularly appears to be going off on a tangent, which only has significance in the context of the course of the process. It also sometimes appears as if nothing is happening and nothing is changing for a long time. Adriaansz and Stijlen recognise the ability to tolerate this apparent standstill as an important attitude in therapy.

An example from Klaasje's course of therapy illustrates this. For weeks she just wanted to work by herself on something for the farewell party of one of the group leaders who was leaving. However, when the music therapist made the connection between the affective significance of the departure of one of the group leaders and the 'departure' of her father, this apparently anomalous, insignificant episode became an extremely valuable one in the whole process.

Which techniques are characteristic of individual therapy?

Klaasje adopted a very non-committal attitude towards music therapy, having initially shown interest in musical instruments in the observation phase. Now she hardly wanted to make music and just found everything stupid. The music therapist accepted her disinclination to use the instruments which he was giving her and temporarily put them to one side. Instead, they made up a song which was about Klaasje coming for music therapy and them making music together. For a long time this song was the opening ritual for each session. Later, a song they made up themselves was added as a closing ritual, so that the departure of Klaasje and the music therapist could be put to song. Although they used to do this together, Klaasje wanted the music therapist to sing it for her, especially the closing song. In this way, she was hearing the affective content of it, but was not herself getting emotionally involved in it. In the closing phase of the therapy this song became increasingly important: Klaasje used to make up verses to it, insisted on singing them alone, alternating with the music therapist, or singing together.

After some months, the music therapist had the impression that Klaasje was going to experience the therapy as an important time. Now and again she brought along a tape with music on it which she herself really enjoyed, and now she also wanted to listen to the music they had made up themselves, which the therapist had been offering to her between the opening and closing songs. Sometimes she addressed the therapist as 'hey, dear', which he interpreted as a sign of intimacy. Coming for therapy usually took place fairly peacefully, but returning to the ward became more and more troublesome for Klaasje. The music therapist then decided to give Klaasje musical instruments again; first, to acquire a bit more room for manoeuvre in the interaction between them both and, second, to get Klaasje to acquire emotional experiences in dealing with the musical tools.

To focus on her feeling of security, he introduced five pentatonically-ordered xylophone blocks, one set for himself and another, the same, for her. He expected these instruments to be safe, as one of the blocks already played a part in the opening song and as the tone was warm and enveloping. 'Shall we make some Chinese music today?' he introduced the music. He himself played whilst Klaasje watched and listened. She did not join in, but light tapping with her left hand indicated involvement. With time, she made her first sounds, which the music therapist embedded in a rhythmical structure. Then, for quite some time, he offered her all kinds of instruments and activities, during which she continually remained in the same musical rut. He followed and strengthened Klaasje in her musical expressions and together they worked on how to make music that is sad, angry, happy, and so on.

Gradually, in different ways, he withdrew more and more from his almost symbiotic attachment to Klaasje giving her the opportunity to separate herself from him. It was a big step forward when she began to play different instruments, but Klaasje became increasingly restless when he no longer followed her all the time. To her horror he even challenged her; for example, by suddenly playing something other than had been arranged. In this way, the concept of separation and departure was involved in the process of therapy: sometimes we make the same music and sometimes we change it about. Sometimes we are together, sometimes we are separated, and sometimes we are 'alone together'.

Even though little was said during therapy, it appeared that Klaasje was still going through a process of emotional change. The bouts of anger on the ward were becoming less frequent; she was now able to hold out reasonably well after a visit from her mother; and changing between playing together and separately did not cause so much tension any more. The changes had, however, to be structured and clear for her: switches which were unexpected and rapid, she would probably always find difficult to deal with. In consultation with the ward, the music therapist decided to round off the therapy. He told her this and encouraged Klaasje to extend the closing song with new verses. One verse was about a baby bear which had to get out of its warm cave and was angry and sad about this at first, but later felt very strong because it seemed able to cope alone and could make friends by itself. After the summer holidays, Klaasje came for therapy once a fortnight and at Christmas the music therapist decided to suggest to Klaasje that they no longer met.

With individual music therapy, the therapist takes his time during all phases. The behavioural potential of the client determines the speed of the therapy. This is necessary, as he will be asked to open himself up emotionally and, in doing so, make himself vulnerable. At the same time, the music therapist endeavours to direct the process of therapy to help the client to reduce his limitations. In doing this, it is important that the therapist creates appropriate conditions for a secure atmosphere. The therapy room must not be too big; there must be a feeling of privacy (for example, no windows onto the corridor where others walk past, no visitors) and it should not look different each time. Offering instruments should not be too overwhelming and the therapist should not overpower the client with his presence (nor with his musical input). It is, perhaps, an obvious prerequisite for a secure atmosphere that there is no time for the therapist's musical or aesthetic standards.

In the same way, it is of prime importance for safeguarding a feeling of safety, that the therapist provides a structure; in other words, that he provides a situation for therapy which is well-organised for the client. He might do this by introducing rituals: a set opening and/or closing song, a set build-up to the session, a constant therapeutic attitude, a clear awareness of the time, and other such considerations.

TECHNIQUES FOR THE BUILD-UP PHASE

It is characteristic of individual music therapy with people with developmental disabilities that the therapist takes the initiative in the first phase. He tempts the client into actually initiating a relationship with himself and with the musical instruments. In seeking the means for contact, he temporarily changes his level of activities: sometimes he is patient, sometimes direct, sometimes questioning, sometimes he gives unprompted answers. This is always combined with as great an acceptance as possible of the client's musical and non-musical expression.

In the first phase, individual techniques come to the fore. In the first place, therapist and client can work together at performing the rituals, as already described. In this way not only safety and structure evolve, but by dint of the fact that they are working together, the fact that the therapist and client are together is also implicitly underlined. Instead of this active method of working, singing or music-making can be ways for the therapist to attempt to break into the client's scope of experience. Not only name songs are suitable, but also songs which are about moving (together). By improvised music-making for the client, the therapist reflects the client's scope of experience and can be allowed to enter into it. This increases the chance of the client accepting the relationship with the music therapist.

TECHNIQUES FOR THE SECOND PHASE OF THERAPY
(WORKING THINGS THROUGH)

When a working relationship has been established, the next phase in the therapy begins. Working through the client's emotional problems is of central importance in this. In Klaasje's case, the development of the therapeutic relationship led to a strong bond between her and the therapist. The feeling of being absolutely safe in her attachment to the therapist was brought more in line with reality in the second phase of the therapy: sometimes the therapist would continue to accompany her playing, but sometimes he would not follow her playing at all. In this way, once again, a process of separation was made tangible to Klaasje, such that she was able (in contrast, however, to other separations) to experience it in a positive way. Now she is able to cope with the idea that, after the (symbolic) separation, being together again will follow, and that her own identity does not depend on her attachment to the therapist.

The essence of the intermediate phase is that, within the safety of the therapeutic relationship and the playing of music, the client is confronted with his own conflicts. It is the essence of music therapy that the conflicting emotional experiences be tackled through the medium of music-making. Problems of aggression, anger control, identity crises – there is hardly any affective problem which cannot be tackled through music therapy (quite apart from the question as to whether music therapy is always the most suitable form of therapy).

There are two major types of technique which the therapist can use in this phase: singing songs and improvised music-making (or even movement). By making up and singing songs, the therapist and the client tackle emotionally-charged themes in a safe atmosphere. Indeed, in their book *Creative Therapy* Grabau and Visser (1987), a description, is given of how a girl, who has been deprived of affection, makes up and sings songs about lonely gypsy children. With the help of movement and music, problems can indeed be ironed out or acted out.

Techniques in which improvised music is made, have in common the fact that interaction between therapist and client plays a central role. This is possible in all techniques in which therapist and client talk to one another by playing instruments: playing together, demonstrating and imitating, the therapist asking questions through the music, which are answered by the client who is himself making music, and so on. Techniques of directing the process of therapy through the client–music relationship and the client–therapist relationship during improvisation sessions have, in particular, been developed at the Middeloo Training Institute. An example of this is the conscious decision to follow up or not to follow up the musical impulses of the client:

- ignoring the undesired musical impulse of the client

- initiating a confrontation by playing something different from his music or by practising another musical option
- emulating the client's playing and playing along with him.

Activities can also be undertaken in which the emotional needs, which are fundamental to the client's problem, are tackled. Examples of these kinds of musical activities are those in which the client is 'powerful' and the therapist is 'submissive', so that the client is able to arrest, ruin or disrupt the musical process, or so that the client is able to be 'small' and let himself be appreciated by the therapist. It is especially these kinds of techniques which can evoke violent experiences on the part of the client, and the therapist will then always use them in a very well-thought-out way, carefully regulate them and then not intensify the experience by not placing limitations to it. One way of adequately resolving violent experiences at the end of a session is by using closing rituals.

TECHNIQUES FOR THE THIRD PHASE OF THE THERAPY
(THE WINDING-DOWN PHASE)

How does the therapist recognise when the therapy can be terminated? On the one hand he is informed by his colleagues in the team conference how they look upon the client's developments; they have, in this respect, mainly got their eye on the manifestation of emotional problems in his actual behaviour. On the other hand, the thought of terminating therapy will only come to mind when the client's problem has been worked through, which will only be the case when the problem has been tackled several times during therapy in different ways, using different affective evocations, and when his experiences are less conflict-ridden or stop being so all together. If we look at the example of Klaasje once more, we see that the fear of separation is worked through in different ways: by dealing with going to and coming from the therapy session; by working at the departure of the group leader; in songs made up by herself about the separation of her parents; by musically improvising with the therapist; and, again, in the way that the therapy is brought to a conclusion.

The winding-down phase can last a long time. As a rule of thumb, it can be expected that it should take just as much time as the build-up phase. The winding-down of the therapy can, at the same time, take place on many levels by:

- making therapy less frequent, leading to a discontinuation of the therapy (for example near a holiday)
- introducing the subject of departure into the therapy, for example by making up songs about it or by thinking up activities
- reducing the intensity of the therapeutic relationship, for example by working on musical activities, creating a musical product on a cassette which the client can take away with him after therapy (this symbolically taking the therapist with him), and so forth.

It is important that the therapist prepares and thinks through the winding-down phase as meticulously as for the other two phases. Much work can be undone because of a termination that is too rapid.

Individual remedial music-making

What reasons may there be for offering individual remedial music-making?

John has, for some four years, attended the adult day care centre. For a long time he was working in a sheltered workshop but, ultimately, this appeared to be too great a strain for him. When he was 34 years old, his parents requested a place at a adult day care centre for him. In the community, John was not very visible. The group leaders continually endeavoured to involve him in group events, but as soon as he saw his chance, he dropped out. Amongst the group leadership a feeling of apathy developed: 'You constantly invest energy to get him involved, but you don't get anything in return!' In the group, John continued not to present many problems: he hardly had any contact with the others and they did not interfere with him. In the team meeting, the suggestion was put forward that the group was possibly too threatening for John. It was often busy and turbulent and the mass of influences appeared to swamp him. It was suggested that John might possibly be given support through music therapy in such a way that he could make more use of the opportunities that the community and the adult day care centre could offer him.

The music therapist interpreted the referral for music therapy in two ways: John appeared to avoid contact with others because he could not cope with this level of contact and, second, it seemed that individual attention was necessary rather than group events. Because the team was of the opinion that, at the moment, a group approach would yield no changes, the opportunity was sought for confronting John alone. But just offering musical activities, in order to meet him in his need for individual attention, appeared to provide too little scope for John to realize his full potential at the adult day care centre. A course of music therapy was also not the obvious choice to make as, besides avoiding social contact, there were few indications of psychological disorders with John. Evading contact seemed to be based more on insecurity about his own abilities and poor self-esteem than on emotional conflicts. The music therapist suspected this because the group leadership did actually find him stable and thought that he was a fairly contented person within his own living environment. For this reason the music therapist opted for a remedial approach.

The crux of remedial music-making is that a form of care is offered in which an attempt is made to influence the client or his environment so that the client's ability to function is improved. The starting point for this form of care lies in the discovery that something is deficient in the client's ability to function. Often the problem with people with developmental disabilities is that they are unable to express themselves, and the question of care must consequently be deduced, by the group leadership and 'experts', from their behaviour. This makes the definition of a problem highly dependent upon the interpretation of the care worker. In the case of John, the team weighed up the decision: 'Do we leave him within his own range of experiences or do we try to get him to share his expereinces of the group?' One of the reasons for actually offering him help was the suspicion that he was probably hankering after contact with others, but did not dare look for it. As well as this, his relatively young age led to the opinion that a broader social perspective would be a desirable thing. He would have to live in the context of the group for many years: first at the adult day care centre, later in a residential institution for the developmentally disadvantaged. The team did not want to run the risk of depriving him of the positive experience of social contact, so long as chances of his fulfilling his potential appeared to manifest themselves. After much deliberation, the decision was made to start offering care.

What, now, are the possible problems which lead to a recommendation for individual remedial music-making? These are generally deficiencies in the client's ability to express himself. They may be limitations which affect the expression of the client: the client is not able to express how he is or how he wishes to be regarded; there might be problems in his relationships with others; the client himself does not dare to express his inner feelings and thought to others. Because he does not feel safe in his relationships with other people, interaction with other people becomes too threatening. In his day-to-day existence, these kinds of problem are recognisable in the form of avoiding contact, feelings of inferiority or very little 'fighting spirit'. These problems all have in common the fact that the client's self-esteem is too weak and this, in turn, is an important indication for remedial music-making.

People with developmental disabilities are, to the same or to a greater extent than the non-developmentally disabled, subject of having poorly developed self-esteem. This is easier to understand if we identify the relationship between the development of self-esteem and the development of a child. The child is, in the first few years of life, already developing his self-esteem. This takes place particularly in his relationship with his parents or those bringing him up, who are able to establish the child's feeling of autonomy and continuity. The child breaks free more and more from his attachment to his parents and increasingly experiences himself as a unit capable of operating self-sufficiently. However, the development of people with developmental disabilities can, in this first phase of life, have its problems. As a result of the disability there can be structural limitations to the potential for development, which make the development of the functional ego more difficult. Examples of these types of limitations for developing into an autonomous unit include:

- deficiencies in motor control which make it more difficult, or impossible, for the child to express himself as a unit capable of operating self-sufficiently (for example not being able to crawl/walk, incontinence, and the like)
- brain damage which imposes limitations on his ability to process influences.

Problems to do with self-esteem can also come about when the separation from the parents and the internal way of way of viewing oneself is not so good. Interaction between parents and child can, for example, cause problems, because the parents may accept their disabled child with difficulty or may be over-protective towards him, as a result of which the development of the child is hindered. It is also possible for parents intuitively to reject the behaviour of their child, for example, if his behaviour is unsettled, aggressively disinhibited, self-injurious or clingy. Fragile or negative self-esteem can result from this.

Now that the indications for offering individual remedial music-making have been described, it is also good to pause for a moment to think about the contra-indications. In essence, there are no reasons why this form of therapy should not be offered. The method has, after all, been indicated so broadly that no diagnostic characteristics can be formulated. The client's attitude towards music can, indeed, be a good reason for turning him down for it. This will be the case if the client rejects music or rigidly adheres to one way of approaching music (for example, playing his own three tunes on his favourite instrument). For some therapists, that constitutes a good reason for not offering remedial music-making. Others, on the other hand, are of the opinion that care must first of all be concerned with changing the client's attitude towards music and that, subsequently, remedial music-making is still possible.

What objectives are pursued in individual remedial music-making?

John had no scruples about getting to know the music therapist. He sympathetically considered the question of whether he liked music. 'Oh yes!' he answered and was silent. The music therapist had planned first of all to use a number of sessions in order to refine the rough objectives. John reacted to the offers of different activities and different instruments by doing was he was asked for a short time and then looking stupidly at the therapist. His look expressed the question: 'Well, is that enough then?' On one occasion he had quite a panic attack when the music therapist wanted to see what happened when a very clear demand was made of him. He asked John to repeat an activity, but this time in the way that the music therapist had demonstrated (that is to say, in his style). After a clear rejection of contact and the fear of failure which was manifested in panic, the music therapist realised that John talked about himself as 'John' and as 'him'. From this he concluded that his avoidance of social contact was rooted in fear: John appeared to be so insecure that others were threatening for him. Expressed in diagnostic terms, his ego-functions were not sufficiently developed and his self-esteem was too fragile, which meant that John saw himself far too little as a person operating self-sufficiently. One possible cause of this was that John had, no doubt continually, had the feeling in his life that he was falling short of the expectations of his parents. Being put into special education from infant school, the only child still to be living at home, and failing at the workshop, are concrete breaking points in his development.

At the same time, the music therapist got the impression that John had developed in a very unbalanced way. His emotional age was very young, although he had a higher level in terms of cognitive and motor abilities at the adult day care centre. The therapist set the following objectives for treating John: first, to strengthen his ego-functions and self-esteem, which in the long run would have to result in increased motivation in establishing contact with the music therapist. After attaining these objectives, the therapist would move on to stimulating his faculties for communication in general, and John's expression in particular. The individual remedial music-making might subsequently be wound down by putting John in a group.

EGO, EGO-STRENGTHENING AND SELF-ESTEEM

As has already been noted, ego-development sometimes runs its course with difficulty. This can lead to a poor functional ego. This is what happened in John's development: he described himself as 'John' or 'him', rather as a two-year-old toddler does. The self-esteem, and consequently the ability to say 'I want' or 'I can', had hardly developed, if it had at all. Because of his efficiency in adapting himself to the expectations of others and his capacity for compensating on a cognitive level, this had not, however, caused any problems for a long time. His emotionally young age had simply not become apparent to others and did not seem to lead to many conflicts for him. Before John's treatment, the music therapist set one objective which was based on a very early age in psychological development.

With this in mind, we come to an important objective in individual remedial music-making (which, for that matter, is usually also important with music therapy): working on ego-strengthening. This involves an aspect other than self-esteem. 'Self-esteem' refers to somebody's experience of being a consistent, competent person, whereas when we talk about working on ego-strengthening, the ego as a functional entity is referred to. The ego is a developing function of the child (as well as the adult), which mediates between its impulses, desires and needs, on the one hand, and the demands of the outside world on the other.

In a volume on the subject of supportive child psychotherapy, Cluckers *et al.* (1986) point out that ego-strengthening is very much a matter of speaking to the client on a level on which he is or ought to be able to function well. By expanding his faculties, conditions can be created for further developing his ego-function. In doing so, it is important to make a distinction between nurturing skills and stimulating development. In the case of training, the child is given practice in something that is unfamiliar to him, something that as yet does not have any significance. In order to encourage ego-development it is, however, necessary for stimulation of the development to take place within the therapist—client relationship and for stimulation of development to come from the client himself (and at the same time, therefore, be of significance to him).

On the basis of this description of Clucker's thought process, it clearly becomes apparent that ego-strengthening is essentially something other than merely rewarding desired behaviour or lavishly and continuously praising the client. An ego-strengthening course of therapy consists of (once again) starting up a developmental process with the client by drawing on what has, up to now, been still-untapped potential. An experience in taking remedial action from everyday practice, in which no systematic form of care ultimately seemed necessary, can make this point clear.

A developmentally disabled resident of a half-way house in the institute suffered from fears (of failure), which were connected to a severely punitive approach to religious standards. Regular discussions with his tutor provided no results, any more than the appeasing observations of the minister from his catechism. There were certainly results from his taking up a new activity (in his case learning to paint), through which he experienced the fact that he did not have to fail and was able to enjoy something nice. At the same time he was stimulated in his community to be more active in participating in cooking, drinking coffee together, and so on. In the course of the years, he became noticeably stronger and developed a more positive self-esteem. The fear of being a sinner who ought to be punished faded into the background (whilst his attendance of a church continued and still does).

In discussing the techniques we will go into more detail on the subject of ego-strengthening.

EXPRESSION AND GROWTH

In daily practice, many music therapists do not set their objectives in terms of ego-strengthening, but form their framework for the use of remedial music-making on the basis of their understanding of the traditions of humanistic psychology. As we said, in the setting of John's objectives, if self-esteem is developed, the potential for expression can also be increased. What is meant by expression here is that John could articulate his feelings, his identity, his desires and needs. This brings us to growth-oriented objectives. It was shown in Chapter One how the self-realization of a person with a developmental disability in his personal relationships with other people becomes an important aspect of care. The aim of the care worker is to develop faculties which put the person with the developmental disability in a position to be able to be himself and express himself as much as possible. It is not generally very easy to make concrete such objectives as self-expression, fulfilling one's potential, self-realization or growth. Yet these are the concepts which we, usually intuitively, are able to point to. When a client undergoes a change from defensive repeated playing to a rhythm, to a confident rhythmical feeling of freedom, we can interpret that as growth in his inner feeling of freedom. Even if a client first wishes to play back well-known television artists and wants to sing later and makes movements he has thought up himself, this can be interpreted as a sign of increased ability to express himself. The changes which are being pursued can also clearly manifest themselves in a new way of interacting with others. This tallies with the point of view that a person with a developmental disability is only able to fulfil his potential in a personal relationship with another person. It is no wonder, then, that many objectives are indeed about communicating with other people.

The order in which the objectives are described has not come about arbitrarily, but is based on factors in developmental psychology. Although the objectives may also be tackled at the same time, developing into an individual is described in this order. Experiencing self-esteem is a fundamental stage in every person's development. When the child knows himself to be an individual, he is able to experience himself as a person operating self-sufficiently and can express himself as such. In his relationships with other people the child, and later the grown-up, can experience consolidation of his self-esteem. The fact that, in his interaction with others, everything can at times go wrong, is another story. When a child does not have this kind of consolidation or denies or distorts any possible consolidation on the basis of his self-esteem, interaction with others can also becomes threatening.

From setting the objectives, it appears to be clear that there is an overlap with individual music therapy. Ego-supporting treatment, for example, is also considered by many as a form of psychotherapy.

What techniques are used in individual remedial music-making?

The meetings with John were characterised by long silences, even though John said that he found making music once a week enjoyable. Singing the opening and closing songs together was becoming a set ritual, which was meticulously upheld by John in the pauses. However, when the therapist suggested a different activity, within three minutes the playing would fizzle out. It quickly became apparent that the music therapist was too active and that, because of this, John was able to remain too passive. The therapist expected reciprocal interaction, yet that was something of which John did not yet feel capable. The music therapist decided to drop their joint improvised music-making for the time being.

For many sessions the music therapist played the guitar and sung songs, whilst John listened and appeared to be enjoying it. Gradually, songs were introduced, in which, in a number of ways, a role was assigned to John as he was listening. The song 'If you're happy and you know it...' was sung, in one song the last word of a few lines was left out, songs with actions were introduced, and so forth. Gradually, singing became a shared experience for John and the music therapist. To emphasise John's individuality, they took it in turns to choose which song should be sung. A 'mistake' which John made whilst singing was picked up by the music therapist. Again and again, the music therapist worked through his impulse to arrive at something new; sometimes jokingly, sometimes seriously, but all the time John could feel that his unexpected attempt was being taken positively and was leading to something 'greater'. In any case, he could clearly see that he himself was making an individual input.

In the following phase of therapy, the music therapist introduced instruments once again, but now with more care: first a drum or a cymbal to accompany a song, then two drums, claves and a few odd xylophone blocks. Once again, playing music went according to the build-up: the music therapist played for John, they played the same thing, they played different things. Anyone listening would have heard that 'John's type of music' was being played predominantly: gentle, somewhat subdued tones with little variation in dynamics and tempo. Later, when it was safe to bring out unexpected features in the instrumental playing, the music became richer in contrast and more erratic. John clearly began to express himself more freely in his use of the musical tools. Sometimes he took up the musical challenge of the music therapist, but sometimes he shook his head: 'No, do it as normal'. Slowly but surely two individuals became audible in the playing. The music therapist gave John support by holding back musically and by mainly following John's playing. In spite of this, a strong interdependence seemed to exist between the therapist and John. If the therapist differed too much in his music or did not give enough support, John would get worried and go quiet. His strength-ened ego, which was becoming so visible in improvisation, had not yet resulted in positive self-esteem. In the case of John, the music therapist decided to let him learn a musical piece. 'How would you like to play our songs together on a recorder?' he asked him. Carefully, the recorder was introduced and he taught John how to play well-known tunes with the help of a colour-code system. In great secrecy, John also practised throughout the week in the corner of his community living area (if the others did not appear to be listening). Great was his surprise and pride when one day in his community 'as if by chance' a familiar song was sung that he could play along to on the recorder. 'The music therapist really should have heard him!' was the report he gave the next day.

After about eighteen months, John's treatment was wound up. In the individual sessions he seemed to feel more and more sure of himself and he gave clear indications to this effect. In his community, however, he changed very slowly; the others still remained at (too great) a distance. Moreover, it did not seem feasible to let John make music in a group: the time available to the therapist was up and John would not fit into the two groups that the music therapist had. The team decided to go ahead with the winding up and to put John in the speech therapist's group for the development of social skills.

John's therapy is just an example of the way in which individual remedial music-making is carried out. There are many different ways of realizing the objectives but, generally speaking, characteristic techniques again and again find a place in this. We will, in fact, discuss a number of them. We will limit ourselves to the techniques which have not already been described in discussing individual music therapy.

BODY-ORIENTED TECHNIQUES

It is sometimes the case with a person with a developmental disability that their body-awareness is under-developed. The person is not sufficiently aware of his body and its place in his environment. It is also possible that he has a false impression of his movements and coordinates them badly: for example, they go off in the wrong direction or he moves with insufficient intensity. This is obviously connected to his bodily feeling, the subjective judgement that each person makes about his own body. Attention is often devoted to the body in remedial music-making. This is hardly surprising, as the body is strongly connected to one's self-esteem. If a child (or a grown-up) is not consciously aware of his body, he is not yet able to separate himself from the outside world. And it is separating oneself from other people which is actually fundamental to having self-esteem. Of course, for music therapists who are working with children with developmental disabilities, body-oriented work commonly features amongst their objectives. Becoming aware of one's body happens in different ways. One point at which to start is by touching parts of the body with a resounding instrument, such as a kettledrum, a cymbal or a tambourine. It is even possible to get the client to lie down between two pianos on a huge sound box, (as is described by Adriaansz (1986)). In such cases, the vibrations from the instrument produce tactile experiences, which direct the client's attention to his body or to a specific part of his body. Similarly, denoting parts of the body, for example by singing songs in which parts of the body are referred to or are moved, also contributes to the development of body-awareness.

The second aspect of body-awareness concerns the use of the body: to what extent can the client successfully plan and carry out his movements? This aspect of motor control and coordination normally belongs to movement or psycho-motor therapy, but music therapists too work a great deal in caring for people with a developmental disability through the medium of movement. Music and movement are actually very closely related to each other. Just as with the discovery of corporality, the discovery of movement is built up from the most fundamental factors. A good example of this is where the therapist holds the client and therapist and client sway together with the music which is being played. However, the therapist can also split up the skin of a drum into sections in which the client has to play and, when making music, to distinguish whether uncontrolled or steady movements are being made to the music. Learning to play an instrument contributes to the development of eye–hand coordination and fine motor control. We will go into this in more detail in discussing group remedial music-making, given that working at motor control appears to be an important objective.

LEARNING MUSICAL SKILLS

As became clear in the description of John's therapy, learning musical skills is used to realize remedial objectives. In the way that this technique is used, an important characteristic of remedial music-making can be recognised. In what way does learning to play an instrument contribute to attaining objectives such as ego-strengthening, encouraging growth or stimulating expression? One important contribution to ego-strengthening is made through the feeling of satisfaction on completion of a difficult task. 'If I can do that, then

I really must be somebody!' might be how such emotions could be translated. Just as it has been said above, ego-strengthening does not take place through the development of skills which are unfamiliar to the client and are consequently meaningless to him (as in a music lesson). The way in which the instrument is taught must then be incorporated into a process experienced by the client; only then can it have any significance.

An example of this is the way in which a marginally psychotic young man came to play the piano. For months on end during sessions it had come up for discussion the way he felt alternately big and small and how he escaped into all kinds of fantasies. The therapist introduced the piano to determine contrasts on the piano: high/low, loud/quiet, each person playing alone/four hands all mixed up. These observations evoked all kinds of feelings in him, especially feelings of fear, which were once again reflected when improvising. After some time had passed, he also wanted to make a note of some kind of improvisation, to remember it and then to be able to reproduce it. His grasp of reality was strengthened. The music therapist also suspected by then that a desire would also follow for him to want to learn to play the piano. When he asked this question, it would be agreed to, and in this way the course of treatment could be wound down.

There are also music therapists who always start with the teaching of an instrument. They usually do so to deal with a concrete question of the client and to prevent the client from having fears by 'occupying him with a structured pursuit'. This way of acting has one major disadvantage and it has probably got more to do with the preferences of the music therapist than thinking out a method. Just as in music therapy, musical and aesthetic standards and values ought to be avoided in remedial music-making. The client must be brought there to make his own, unique music and to experience this as a reflection of himself. Learning to play an instrument is, however, inextricably linked with standards: this is how it must be played, these are the notes, this is how the instrument sounds on record, and so forth. Not only are imperceptible standards included in the therapy in this way, but the feeling of security can also be reduced. The chance he will fail, he will not fulfil his own and other people's expectations now increases sharply.

Conclusion

In this chapter the background to opting for an individual course of treatment and methods of individual music therapy and individual remedial music-making were described.

In everyday practice, a music therapist will rarely limit himself strictly to one of the two methods. Ego-strengthening, in the form that it is described in individual remedial music-making, essentially has a role to play in music therapy as well. Similarly, the client–therapist relationship or the client–music relationship can very well be employed in remedial music-making. Sometimes these different elements as regards method actually find a place at the same time in the treatment, and sometimes they are used one after the other. In this way, for example, body-oriented techniques can in several ways be used in treatment in music therapy with a client with a poorly-defined identity: in the first phase as a means of establishing contact, in the intermediate phase when the ego is strengthened, or at the moment at which the experience of self-esteem has been worked through. A combination of both methods, by using them one after another, can be seen in learning an instrument at the end of a course of music therapy or in the first phase of body-oriented work in remedial music-making with a child. May the reader be thus warned (again) against too dogmatic an attitude. Therapeutic practice calls for a flexible anticipation of the need for help. The essence of the distinction between music therapy and individual remedial music-making is partly that the therapist himself takes responsibility for the methodical path which he chooses to walk: why is one of the methods indicated, what results can realistically be expected and which techniques ideally contribute to attaining the objectives?

CHAPTER FOUR

Group Treatment

When should group treatment be offered?

This question is as difficult to answer as the question covered in the last chapter, of why individual treatment is chosen. The intuition of the therapist and the team members has a large role to play in the choice in favour of group treatment. The client's interest in music is more of a consideration for making a recommendation than in individual therapy. A very positive attitude towards music can constitute a good reason for the team to offer the opportunity of making music in a group. This kind of reasoning does have one clear advantage: it is the client who is expressing the motivation. On the other hand, this kind of indication does not say anything: offering a course of treatment because the client finds the medium attractive does not mean that the objectives are set methodically and logically.

The same problem arises whenever the choice of this form of treatment is greatly determined by practical considerations.

Practical considerations

The therapist's available time in relation to the total number of residents or participants of the institution is often very limited. In his range of responsibilities, the therapist must create room on the one hand for team conferences and reports and on the other for both individual and group treatment. In an institution it is normal for a music therapist to have a hefty number of hours to his schedule, but the number of residents he sees is proportionately large, whilst at a child day care centre or at an adult day care centre he will often only have three to six available hours a week. Consequently, the music therapist balances out his time and makes the necessary choices. A team can decide that everybody should make music every week, as that is thought of as valuable for every resident or participant. Sometimes the plan for treatment might also look as if all activities should take place in the day time group, or with the day time group. In both cases the whole of this group is put down on the schedule for music.

With both ideas about treatment, this can be qualified in three ways. Of course it is preferable that each resident or participant has the chance of making music; it is just a question of whether the expertise of the music therapist is always necessary for this. Other ways of using music are also possible, and these can be organised by an activity supervisor or a group leader (possibly under the supervision of the music therapist). These types of activity are described in Chapter Two, under musical activities. Another qualification has to do with the objectives which can be pursued with a referral, determined by a detailed schedule. Although the community can be put together in a group on the basis of clear considerations, the individual objectives for the members of the group usually differ greatly. Sometimes a fairly uniform group can work out well, but it is also possible that the individual objectives within the music group differ too greatly. Then the therapist only pursues very general objectives, such as deriving pleasure from making music, for example, and even developing self-confidence by doing so. The essence of what is set out above is that the choice in favour of a practical way of making a referral with a detailed schedule has direct consequences for the scope of the treatment.

The third, and final, qualification relates to the choice made on principle in favour of group treatment rather than individual treatment. It is the writer's impression that, in caring for people with developmental disabilities, an individual approach is sometimes avoided (this particularly appears to be the case in child day care centres and adult day care centres). A day care centre is not, after all, a place for treatment, is how the argument usually goes. This book is probably not the place to go into the differences of approach towards treatment, but it can be put forward that an exclusive recommendation for group music-making does not do justice to the fact, borne from experience, that sometimes an individual approach is better and for this reason is preferable. A therapist who, in his institution, exclusively works in groups, should be able to confirm whether this is as a direct result of evasive behaviour or whether there are substantive reasons to support his choice. In the last case, on the basis of a range of considerations, the experts are able to decide upon some kind of delegation of responsibilities: individual courses of treatment, for example, are carried out by the movement therapist or the psychologist/remedial educationalist, whilst the music therapist and the speech therapist are in charge of the courses of group treatment.

Besides the practical considerations, specific problems of the client can also suggest that a group approach would be beneficial: problems with social skills, problems of a cognitive nature and of a motor control nature.

Problems with social skills

People with developmental disabilities who live in institutions spend the largest part of their time in groups: day-time community groups, activity groups, the dormitory group, the group from the bus which takes them each day to the day care centre and the group with which they go on holiday. When the groups are put together the individual may have little influence over this decision generally, whilst at the same time the choice to continually live in close proximity with others is usually not a free choice. The social skill of interacting with others in a group is for this reason of tremendous importance.

In order to remain oneself and not to get lost in the group, it is important that somebody is sufficiently ego-strong and has positive self-esteem. If that is the case, then he will look upon himself as a person who exists independently alongside others. In Chapter Three we already stated that, if there is a severe disorder in an individual's capacity to communicate, an individual course of treatment is offered to start with. However, there can also be other, less serious problems in the way they interact with others. Examples of this include:

- avoidance of contact or insufficient awareness of other people's presence
- a lack of actual faculties for communicating with other people, such as a speech impediment, a language disorder or a physical disability which limits the possibilities for expression.

Problems of a cognitive nature

An important type of learning is learning from experience: by doing something himself or by observing others, a person can acquire new skills. One condition for learning by observation is that one is in a position to direct one's attention towards something and then to retain this. If the ability to concentrate is impaired, then that is an indication that group music therapy would be beneficial. Other cognitive-oriented indications include, for example, lacking eye–hand coordination or deficient processing abilities of audial, visual or tactile perception.

Problems with motor control

In Chapter Three it was already noted that, in most institutions for people with developmental disabilities, movement therapists probably also work there, but that at the same time music therapists often work in a body-oriented way. From this, a rough distinction can be made between two approaches. On the one hand the natural link between music and movement is exploited. Group remedial music-making is offered if the client has defective general motor control, which is in no way connected to a lack of bodily-awareness.

Examples of this include athetoid[1] motor control, inhibited motor control, repeatedly bumping oneself, a bad sense of balance, and the like. On the other hand, the link between playing an instrument and the movement which is necessary to make the music, is exploited. If this is the case, music-making is actually the form in which developing motor control is wrapped up. One indication is that the fine motor control is impeded, whether it be as a result of an organically-induced disability or as a result of a lack of stimulation. In more concrete terms, one might think, for example, of the use of the fingers or eye–hand coordination.

Reasons for not offering group treatment

The first consideration for not offering group treatment logically arises out of the reason first stated for actually offering it: if the client rejects music, group music-making is a less obvious option. If it is work with children, such as at a child day care centre, this consideration plays less of a role than with adults with developmental disabilities. Children's attitudes towards music are even less determined by standards and value systems than those of adults.

A methodical consideration for not offering group treatment can be the severity of the client's problems. The more serious the client's problems are, the more obvious an option is individual treatment by means of music therapy or remedial music-making. The eventuality of the group being too threatening or too chaotic for the client must be avoided. In such an instance he would be more likely to regress than to make any progress. This brings up the question of whether it is actually possible to offer group treatment in the form of music therapy (and consequently as a form of psychotherapy). It might be loosely put forward that an important constituent part of group psychotherapy is (introspectively) reflecting on one's individual experiences and those of others. With people with developmental

---

1   'Athetosis': damage to the ganglia causes frequent involuntary movements interfering greatly with normal movements of the body.

disabilities it is not usually possible to achieve this kind of introspection: the level of psychological development of most is not such as to be able to do this. Pursuing a psychotherapeutic process of change by means of a group approach is, in this case, hardly, if at all, possible. The methods for group treatment which will now be discussed are also, for the most part, methods on the level of remedial music-making. Some characteristics of care in the form of musical activities will indirectly come up for discussion.

Remedial music-making as a means of developing social skills

What problems are appropriate for referral?

Everybody in the adult day care centre knew Miranda. More than that, from the way she spoke, it was impossible not to know her. Whoever came into the day care centre, could hear her chattering or grumbling and swearing. Miranda seemed to be everywhere and this impression was felt three times as strongly in the day time group. In a busy, somewhat compulsive way, with her loud voice, she continually demanded attention from the group leadership and was always commenting on the behaviour of others. Her frequently changing moods did not make it easy to build up a consistent way of interacting with others: sometimes Miranda was irritatingly critical, disruptive and offensive; sometimes she was irritatingly euphoric, smoochy and clingy. However, if she were not exemplifying one of these two patterns of behaviour, then the group leadership got the impression that she hardly had any contact with others and was essentially a shy person.

During the team discussion, a substantial amount of time was spent on Miranda's behaviour. Above all, working with her was troublesome for the group leadership because she showed so many feelings of rejection towards them. They also found it difficult to draw the line with her in a secure atmosphere, as they had no insight into Miranda's abilities: what kind of an influence did her brain damage have? Were there emotional problems? Was she lacking a sense of and the actual skills for interacting with other people? For the time being these questions could not be given any unequivocal answer, but the members of the team were agreed that something must be done. Miranda was in danger of losing contact with the members of the group and a disproportionate amount of the group leadership's time was taken up with her. For this reason, the team decided to put Miranda for three months in the 'social skills group'. Should the music therapist suspect that she could profit from this time, then the team could make the referral for a longer period of time.

From the outside, Miranda does not appear to have any problems interacting with others: she is always able, in her own way, to establish contact (usually in an angry or cheerful mood). However, if we take our own experience of her behaviour seriously, there do indeed appear to be definite problems. Her talking is euphoric or aggressive and she evokes in others feelings of wariness. If she does not have the protection of her moods, she seems hardly to be able to establish any contact. One important criterion in offering remedial music-making is the qualitative experience of social interaction. In this, too, the interpretation of the care worker once again plays a large role. The care worker can assess from his own observations what the need for help is or can seek the advice of others; how do they look upon contact with the client? This interpretation is mainly directed towards the question of how the client himself looks upon contact with other people. One criterion is, for example, whether making contact is satisfying or frustrating. One question that the therapist can himself ask is: is the client, in playing together with other people, evoking positive reactions or is he rather creating individual rejection? Remedial music-making offers the client an opportunity to discover and subsequently establish new ways of interacting with others.

AVOIDING CONTACT

Miranda's diagnosis also points in the direction of other, directly related problems. It is not just a matter of her strict method for establishing contact, but also how she avoids contact with others. If she is not excessively cheerful or angry, she avoids the others and appears to be a vulnerable soul. A second group of indications is made up of this kind of contact problems:

- not feeling capable of establishing contact with other people

- having too limited an awareness of the presence of others.

If it appears that the client does not feel capable of establishing contact with others, the problem is one of fearing other people. He feels threatened and avoids contact, for example, because he has feelings of inferiority, is burdened by the fear of failure, or does not have much of a fighting spirit. Sometimes, in everyday language-usage, this type of contact-avoiding behaviour is called autistic-like behaviour. It should be noted that autism, a psychiatric disorder, constitutes an indication for individual music therapy.

The second type, a limited awareness of other people, can find its cause in the emotional age of the client. In terms of psychological development he could be compared with a child of less than two years old. The client is, 'as is normal', not yet aware of other people (in terms of playing: it is mainly a matter of parallel playing). Remedial music-making endeavours to get the client to become aware of the presence of other people and to motivate him to make contact with them.

LACKING SOCIAL SKILLS

One final, and very obvious indication for group remedial music-making is a lack of communication capabilities. Sometimes a person with a developmental disability does not experience any emotional problems in making contact with other people, but his interaction with others is not without difficulties as he does not have enough social skills, such as, for example:

- being able to fit into a group

- waiting your turn

- working together on the making of a 'product'

- being capable of mutual interaction.

What objectives can be pursued?

Miranda's first acquaintances with the group went just as the music therapist expected. The four members of the group were all long beforehand informed by Miranda of her imminent arrival and the welcome was extremely hearty. Miranda tried to conceal her insecurity by directly taking the lead: 'Are we going to start now, what are we going to do, are we going to make music?' The group was quite bewildered, but the music therapist encouraged William to explain the opening ritual. The first one in the circle took two claves out of a box and rhythmically tapped along to the song, which was about him being there. Following this, it was the next person's go and, consequently, two names were sung. Finally, all six people had claves and their name was sung, one after the other. At the end of the session this was done in reverse order with a closing song.

It became apparent to the music therapist how insecure Miranda was and how much difficulty she had in integrating into group activities. She was continually making observations, laughing loudly, issued criticism about the playing of somebody else and twirled restlessly on her chair. In brief, she was a disruptive factor in the group and without a match. The others scarcely reacted to her and did not appear to be listening. They were aware of her behaviour and she did not usually have much to say. Her isolation was noticeable. First of all the music therapist adopted a reserved attitude and offered Miranda and the old members of the group protection by working to a rigid structure. Miranda's behaviour was the same that month during the other three sessions as well.

On the basis of his observations and the considerations of the team, the music therapist then set two, equally important objectives. Miranda did not appear herself to be able to give form and structure to the many influences which were imposed upon her. By continually reacting to different influences it was not sufficiently possible for her to feel stable enough to initiate balanced relationships. The first objective was to get her to experience structure and to teach her to create this herself. The intermediate objectives in this were: to get her to experience structure created by others; to get her to be able to function 'socially' within a definite structure; to increase her concentration span; and to create structure herself in a musical activity. The second objective was to get Miranda to experience a mutual relationship with other people. These objectives were linked to the established isolation in which Miranda found herself in the presence of other people. The intermediate objectives which were set in this included: being aware of one another; listening to one another; and working towards mutual interaction.

The problems in relation to social skills can be summed up in three questions:

- Is the client aware that there are other people?

- Does the client wish to establish contact with others and how does he find relationships with others?

- Does he have sufficient resources to form and maintain relationships?

These questions lead on to the setting of the following objectives.

BECOMING AWARE OF ONESELF AND OF OTHERS

In Chapter Three, in which the methods for individual courses of treatment are set out, much attention is devoted to strengthening self-esteem. Yet this is not only an area for individual treatment. If sufficient ego-strength is available, a group approach is sometimes used to continue to expand the self-esteem. It is in interacting with others that this is, in fact, strengthened. Each person's development process starts with one's attachment to parents and one's environment, via a separation process, and on to a feeling of existing alone and being able to function as an independent person. In a group, the aspect of separation and the experience of attaching oneself without merging with the others takes shape in many forms. It is clear that this is not possible with severely disabled people and is not possible with young children with a developmental disability. They still do not perceive any difference between the inside and the outside world and some will never be able to do so.

Realizing this objective usually occurs through a number of intermediate objectives:

- becoming aware of one's individual presence in the group
- learning to express oneself in the group
- becoming aware of the presence of others in the group
- experiencing a sense of community
- experiencing the differences between oneself and other people.

MOTIVATING THE CLIENT TO ESTABLISH CONTACT

From the description of Miranda's behaviour it is clear that she was hankering after contact, but there were many obstacles to overcome. The reasons for avoiding contact with others can vary greatly. The long period of physical abuse by her father definitely played a role for Miranda. For others, the outside world does not have to be tangibly daunting, but one's experience of it can be (might have been) frightening. People with developmental disabilities sometimes struggle with negative self-esteem as time and again they come up against the limitations of their capabilities in their life. For some people, accepting their disability is a great problem. Illustrations of these types of problem are, for example, the fear of failing, feelings of inferiority or insecurity. Whoever cannot accept himself will also have difficulty in accepting others or in making contact with them. Remedial music-making endeavours to get the client to experience how establishing and keeping up contact does not have to be threatening. Besides accepting the disability, the ego-feeling can also change for the better as a result of this.

FINDING NEW WAYS OF ESTABLISHING CONTACT

Miranda had found her own way of coming into contact with others. She avoided any real closeness by giving form to her relationships with others in fairly rigid ways (aggressively or euphorically). Each person, on the basis of his desires, needs and fears, develops his own way of interacting with others. With Miranda, her way was probably inadequate (in the long run), but she was so bound up in it that she did not know of any other way of acting. One important objective is to encourage the client, in a safe atmosphere, to find new ways of establishing contact and then to strengthen these. As has already been put forward in Chapter Three, in doing this it is, above all, important to bring out the client's individuality. Strengthening small impulses that come from the client himself is more important than teaching ways of interacting with others that are initiated by the therapist. The therapist still actually offers 'interactional models': basic patterns according to which forms of interaction between people can be realised. Examples of types of mutual interaction include lead-ing/following, waiting for one another, working together, and so forth. The client can, through many musical techniques, develop his own way of interacting with other people.

What techniques are used to develop social skills?

The opening ritual immediately created considerable problems for Miranda. She could hardly bear the pressure of waiting her turn. In irritation she incited everyone to hurry up: 'Hey, come on!' The music therapist made sure that he was sitting next to her in the subsequent sessions during the opening and closing songs. He even put his hand on her arm when she gasped for air to be able to shout and said to her: 'Hey, waiting is difficult if you really want to join the group.' At the time that Miranda came into the group there was a lot of improvisation, with one person after the other taking the lead. This person was able to say when the others were allowed to play or when they had to stop. For the time being this was dropped, as a new member of the group came along.

For a number of months the group mainly made music in a circle and the music therapist's used such techniques as 'passing on' a short rhythm played on claves, very quietly singing a song into your neighbour's ear and then getting the song to go around the circle. A great impression was made on Miranda, especially when everyone played the rhythm, one after the other, that she had invented. She was actually astonishingly quiet during this and then let out the tension in a laughing fit. This seemed to be a good approach and many variations of this theme followed on: everybody imitates what one person is doing. In this way both rhythmical patterns and movements are imitated, but it was also possible for two members of the group to imitate one another or two smaller groups to imitate each other in pairs. In this way Miranda was made aware of others and she was able to react to others in a safe way ('So I only have to imitate him?' she asked in disbelief). The fact that others were imitating her boosted her ego-feeling enormously: there was some-body who was observing her and was finding what she was doing important! In this way and other ways, work was done to make her aware of her own presence in the group and that of others.

In the course of time, this relatively structured form of music-making was reorganised into more open forms of music-making. Instead of imitating one another, now a personal reaction to other people's music was being called for. First of all the music therapist asked Carla to make music and said to Miranda: 'Miranda, Carla is now going to play a piece of music for you. Do you also want to play something for her afterwards?' He then asked the others in the group what they had heard in the playing. The choice of instruments slowly changed with time. Gradually, the claves, triangle and tam-bourine were replaced by drums, xylophone blocks and a xylophone. It was considerably easier for Miranda to wait for somebody who was playing for her specially than to listen to two other people who were playing together. However, by then, there was a definite part of the group which was going to break off and the others would not accept her criticism and unexpected incitements any more: 'Keep your hair on, you stupid idiot!' The music therapist actively inter-vened in the case of foul language, but for the rest, made frequent use of the corrective possibilities which the group offered Miranda. On the one hand, he provoked her to offer resistance to the others and, on the other, he articulated those kinds of corrective observa-tions in terms of general rules. He made observations such as: 'William says that each person's playing is equally important and that we have to listen to each one!' or 'Sometimes we chat with each other, sometimes we listen to one another.' Miranda was now taken seriously and accepted as a member of the group (offered some safety), but also experienced serious resistance, which had been impossible in the past.

In the description of Miranda's therapy a number of important techniques stand out. Some people are more aware of the individual, seen in such things as listening to others or bringing structure into music oneself (for example, having a build-up or being able to stop), but techniques are also used which affect the direct interaction between members of the group, such as passing on rhythms in a circle, reacting to somebody else or making music together. As for what instruments the therapist uses, he will always give thought to the processes which are at work in every group. We are not just recognising helpful factors, but processes in group dynamics as well. We will now look at a number of techniques.

PLAYING MUSIC TOGETHER

A very obvious technique for developing social skills is improvised music-making in a group. With the help of these techniques, objectives can actually be pursued such as:

- becoming aware of oneself and others
- getting motivated to initiate contact
- finding new ways of establishing contact.

The different intermediate objectives are continually being realised with the help of other techniques. Consequently, an opening ritual is important for becoming more aware of oneself and of others in the group, just as was done in the case of Miranda. Activities in a circle, such as passing on a rhythm, direct the attention of the group participants more and more onto oneself and others. Other activities, geared towards groups of two people, include: leading and following, asking and answering, activities with dialogue or imitating one another. To do this, percussion instruments in particular can be used, such as claves, tambourines, odd xylophone blocks, and the like.

Working towards improvised playing in a group is a good build-up on the part of the institution towards improvising to an instruction. The way this works is first of all by entrusting the participants with different instruments and investigating how they use them. One possibility is for the therapist to play the instrument with the individual clients in turn, before letting them play together. At the beginning, the therapist will give a rigid structure to everybody's playing by setting a theme, (for example, going from loud to soft and back to loud again), by giving instructions, by giving a signal for starting and for finishing, and so on. When the group is familiar with this and feels safe, the therapist gradually endeavours to get the clients themselves to introduce the structure. Possible activities following this might be that one member of the group is the leader and the others follow, or that an improvisation is thought out and carried out by the group.

WORKING TOWARDS A PROJECT OR A THEME

One widely-used working method for developing social skills is working on a project, for example by producing a lasting product together, such as an audio tape, a film/video or a so-called sound library. Other possible approaches are: thinking up a musical fantasy game together (playing at being Chinese), adding to the text of existing songs with one another through the medium of music, or practising a ready-made musical performance together. Depending on how the group is put together, there are two organisational choices with these techniques. It is possible for the therapist to work out in one year individual projects or themes and (in consultation with the team or the group leaders) to put a new group together in chunks. At the same time, aspects, for example, of the theme or project can be worked out by the group leaders in the day time groups. However, it is also possible for this technique to be incorporated into the context of on-going group treatment. Choosing one of the two options has important ramifications.

With this technique we come to the interface between working in a product-oriented way and a process-oriented way (and the difference between remedial music-making and musical activities). With these kinds of techniques work is being done on a definite product, whilst at the same time the process of acquiring social skills is being stimulated. A rule of thumb in this is that, if aiming for a product conflicts with aiming for a process, then the therapist should subordinate the completion of the product to the process of developing the client or the group. The basis for this lies at the start of the project: the therapist can offer the group a clearly defined plan or draft a plan with them. In practising a musical performance which has been designed by somebody else, developing social skills is a very valuable additional phenomenon in working at a product collectively (this is considered as a type of musical activity). Drafting and working out a plan together, however, gives the therapist many possible ways of controlling the process, despite being geared towards a final product. The therapist can attach great value to the personal input of the client and sometimes decide, on the spot, to devote the session to this purpose. In this way he is encouraging the personal initiative of the client.

When working towards a theme, product-orientation is usually more common than with a project. In this case too, the basis principle is that the therapist chooses, discusses and gives form to the theme with the clients. Exploring facets of the theme 'autumn' or 'sound' gives the members of the group the chance to express themselves within the group and to experience a sense of communality or dissimilarity. The therapist structures the session in such a way that there is room for the individual experience of the client. This will not happen if an interpretation is given of how to experience the theme beforehand, but the individual experience of each client can be brought out, for example by means of musical improvisation, in which the client expresses his experience of 'autumn'. It is also possible to improvise collectively on the theme: autumnal music versus summer music, wilting versus blossoming, and so on.

MOVEMENT-ORIENTED TECHNIQUES

In this book it has been said earlier that work with music and movement often go together. This is also the case when working on social skills and is especially the case for techniques in which no fixed, prescribed movements are made. Just as with instruments, rhythms can be passed on, for example by squeezing a rhythm in each other's hand. Activities using dialogue are also possible, such as leading and following in movement, or imitating each other. Moving together to music, which has been made up oneself, evokes a strong sense of communality, especially if each person is making the same movement. In relation to movement, just as it was the case for music, it is generally applicable that the movements which the client himself incorporates contribute more to the realization of the objective than movements that the therapist introduces.

Remedial music-making and the stimulation of motor and cognitive skills

What problems are appropriate for referral?

For two years ten-year-old Pascal had been visiting the child day care centre. His parents had surrounded him at home with love and attention, but recognised that at home Pascal was exclusively dependent upon his parents and had little company. When a place became free for Pascal at the child day care centre, they snatched the opportunity with both hands. On account of his severe brain damage, Pascal was confined to a wheelchair and needed a lot of care. Making contact seemed to be very burdensome. Mother and father probably understood him perfectly, but for the group leadership his uncontrolled movements, the sounds from his throat and glances were still, on the whole, meaningless. For this reason, evaluating his functional age was also extremely awkward: did this mean that others did not understand him and he did not understand them? Did this also mean that he did not do or say anything and that he was not able and did not want to do anything? For the time being there were all too many question marks.

In the team discussions these questions were brought up again by the team leadership and the experts. It was clear that something had to happen, as otherwise Pascal was in danger of losing the contact with his group colleagues which he had started to establish. Lacking in any unequivocal indication the team decided upon the following. Because up to then there had been some ambiguity as to his learning abilities, it seemed sensible, in any case, to stimulate Pascal very specifically into speaking. The team speech therapist, when asked, said that up to now in her weekly chat she had been able to find few points of contact. It was thereupon decided to offer Pascal remedial music-making and to put Pascal in the motor control group. In this group of three people were also Gerry (who was also in a wheelchair), Tim (who was paralysed down one side) and a group leader.

The referral for remedial music-making was essentially very broad for Pascal. Social problems in his community (such as being left by the wayside) were pressing, there were speech problems and motor problems and on top of these there were many question marks over his retarded development. It is very often the case now, that with motor problems other problems also exist. Without a doubt, these, too, would be touched on in the treatment. However, to avoid any ambiguity we will concentrate first of all just on the motor and cognitive problems and will treat them as if they were isolated problems. One important aspect of motor problems is that treatment of them belongs first and foremost to the department of movement therapy. At the same time, it is such that, in practice, many music therapists also work in a way which is geared towards using move-ment. We will now look in more detail at how, in practice, it is generally the following conditions which are referred for this method of remedial music-making.

SPEECH DISORDERS

Pascal did not speak, but he did make sounds. To someone who did not know him well, he could scarcely be understood. This meant a serious obstruction to his development. Learning speech and lan-guage is first and foremost probably an indication for speech therapy, but working at the voice and sounds also takes place within remedial music-making.

A closer distinction is made in the diagnosis. There might be problems with speech, which are distinct from language problems and which are caused more by the processing of sound and the use of the voice. One objective, which centres on this kind of problem, might be making the client receptive to auditory influences, or encouraging imitations of sounds from the child. There is another type of speech and language disorder which is connected to an emotional block. If that is the case, the objective might be 'developing emotional expression', and exploring the emotional problems.

WHEN BODILY AWARENESS IS FAIRLY OR COMPLETELY UNDERDEVELOPED

In the chapter on individual treatment, the significance of deficient bodily awareness and negative bodily feeling has already been discussed. Limited awareness of one's own body, its place in its environment or its motor (in)capabilities can make the client very insecure. Bodily awareness is probably also poorly developed with Pascal as well: to have to perceive the world from the seat of a wheelchair will definitely be an element which has a great deal of influence on this. In the discussion of the techniques, we will go into more detail as to the ways in which bodily awareness is worked upon.

DEFECTIVE OR UNDEVELOPED MOTOR CONTROL

People with developmental disabilities usually struggle with motor problems or disorders. For some the disorders are so severe that they are referred for help to services for people with a dual disability, whilst for others motor problems exist. Examples of clients' motor problems, in institutions which are not equipped for people with a dual disability, are spasms and stereotypical types of behaviour. It is important here also to make a distinction between problems which are primarily attributed to the disability and problems which can be ascribed to a retarded development. The more they are attributable to organic causes, the more appropriate is functional training of the affected parts of the body. However, if there are problems with motor control as a result of insufficient stimulation or as a result of emotional problems, strengthening the individual motor impulses is a more appropriate method. Practical examples of possible indications include an athetoid, inhibited gait, neglect to the palsied left-hand side of the body, deficient eye-hand coordination, no orientation reflex, and the like.

CONCENTRATION DISORDERS

A recurrent problem with people with developmental disabilities is that their capacity to process different influences and impulses has been affected. In other words, they lack the ability to synthesise incoming impressions sufficiently. In everyday life, this manifests itself in volatility, so that it seems as if the client is continually jumping from one subject to another. He only remembers information which is given to him in a very structured way, does not himself see the connection and forgets things very quickly. Many of these patterns of behaviour are also related to defective concentration. If the client finds it difficult to concentrate, many things surpass his mental grasp. This is a good reason for offering remedial music-making.

What objectives can be pursued?

Before Pascal came into the group, the music therapist took the time to meet him briefly for half-an-hour a week for four months. He hardly knew him, having just seen him in the corridors and the community, and wanted, first of all, to build up a secure means of contact with him. Moreover, he had to assess what Pascal did or did not want and exactly where the problems now lay. In the first few sessions the music therapist made music for him: he sang songs with Pascal's name in them, he played the piano or got him to listen to percussion instruments and tympany instruments. Pascal's palsied arm was making stronger movements when he listened to music and the music therapist presumed that he sensed they were doing something special together. In the subsequent sessions, the music therapist gave him a drum stick in his left hand and himself knocked it with a cymbal or got Pascal's hand to fall onto the cymbal from a short height. In this way he hoped to get Pascal to experience the fact that he too could make sounds and so elicit a means of contact with him. This seemed to be happening all too painfully little.

After three of the four months that the music therapist had set aside for getting to know him, he began to get a greater sense of what Pascal's reactions were. The palsied arm seemed to be a good barometer for his involvement, but the music therapist could not gauge whether this was a pleasant or unpleasant source of excitement. Even throwing the drum stick away, rather than dropping it out of his hand, the music therapist interpreted as a positive sign; he was also able to express 'no'. In the month which was left, the music therapist indicated the falling of the drum stick by decreasing the pitch of his voice and encouraged him to make his own throat sounds. For the time being this was too great a step and Pascal would not be invited to do this. On the basis of his observations in these four months, the music therapist drew his conclusions and set his objectives: 'It is possible to get Pascal to make meaningful movements and this ought to be consolidated. At the same time he wants to be surrounded by others without himself being active. In the group, attempts must first be made at offering Pascal the kind of situations in which he can react to a sound stimulus in a playful way, if it went unnoticed, with his own sound. After this a self-controlled voice activity might be possible.'

A great variety of skills fall under the heading motor skills. The divergence in the referrals have already been shown. Now that we are coming to the discussion of the objectives, this comes up once again. The music therapist can start at the motor level of development and, on the basis of the objective 'strengthening bodily awareness', can work on mats on the ground, but he can also choose to offer Pascal as much safety in his own emotional living environment as possible and can also just hug him. Finally, he can also put factors in developmental psychology to one side and take the active practising of speech and language as an objective. If we are talking about motor skills, once again we are coming to the distinction, touched upon earlier, between strengthening behaviour which comes from the client himself, and teaching new skills. Both aspects must be tackled if the therapist wishes to improve the motor control. Sometimes it is necessary to offer the client new patterns of movement and to practice these with him. Even the planned stimulation of speech to a large extent consists of teaching, in which music actually is the way in which this is wrapped up. In other aspects of motor control, the client's experience is again of central importance, and bringing out his own impulses is indeed important. When looking at the different objectives we will be tackling this subject.

DEVELOPING OR STRENGTHENING BODILY AWARENESS AND BODILY FEELING

For people with developmental disabilities, just as for people without a developmental disability, the incidence of lacking motor coordination, or athetoid motor control does occur. Sometimes it is not clear whether this is caused primarily by the disability. Often the fear of failing and insecurity have a role to play in one's perception of the outside world. The body does its job in its gentle and then later frantic conquest of obstacles. The body does not then function as a haven of security and the person with the developmental disability does not develop sufficient bodily awareness.

The development of bodily awareness is an important objective in remedial music-making, which can be realised by means of a number of intermediate objectives. By far the most fundamental thing is to be aware that you have a body, in terms of developmental psychology, through the awareness that the body consists of many parts. Getting to know the structure of the body layout and experiencing the different possibilities for each part can be a specific intermediate objective. The following intermediate objective also contains both aspects of learning and of experiencing: the client can explore space through movement tasks, he can see how his body works and what his capabilities are. Through this combination of learning and experience, bodily feeling can positively change for the better or else the physical disability may finally be accepted.

ENCOURAGING SPEECH AND/OR LANGUAGE

Pascal's absence of speech was noticeable. In terms of psychological development, his ability to imitate sounds was less than that of a one-year-old. If, with him, it was just a question of retarded development, that would point to a very young functional age as regards motor development. The spasms in his right arm indicate a disorder in the left-hand side of the brain, which is supposedly standing in the way of spontaneous speech development (speech is always located in the left-hand side of the brain). Spontaneously learning to speak has, as a result, not been sufficiently activated. In this instance too, the therapist makes a rough decision between teaching skills, which are unfamiliar to the client, and developing skills from the impulses of the client himself. To encourage speech, diverse intermediate objectives are set. We should also note that, before the therapist stimulates speech, he ought to check (have it checked) that the hearing of the client is sufficiently intact. If the therapist suspects that there is a retarded development, he first of all attempts to elicit imitations of sounds and noises. How working with your body and using your voice are important in this, is set out in the discussion of the techniques. If the imitation of sounds has already started to occur, it is also then possible to stimulate the development of speech in combination with language. If this is the case, referral to speech therapy can obviously be weighed up as a possibility. However, another point concerns the objective which logically arises out of retardation of speech, possibly because of emotional problems. In such a case it is probably better to offer individual remedial music-making. Similarly, if a group approach is indicated, objectives for expression are above all to be aimed for. Extensive discussion should be devoted to this point. In such a case, apart from verbal communication, attention is devoted to facets of non-verbal communication such as body language and facial expressions.

The more the speech and language retardation seem to be induced by an organic affliction, the more appropriate learning-oriented objectives are. The therapist then devotes his attention to factors such as articulation, and the volume and pitch of his speech. The following objectives can then, for example, be set: training in oral motor control and the control of breathing as a basis for speech, practising articulation, or increasing both passive and active vocabulary.

STIMULATING MOTOR CONTROL

With Pascal, it was not just a matter of limited bodily awareness, but also of limited motor activity. The therapist decided to activate motor activity directly by getting Pascal's movements to be meaningful, for example by getting him to make sound with the drum stick in his falling hand. Now we are principally coming to the learning-oriented approach of motor problems and disorders. Possible objectives are:

- stimulating movement of the upper body and arms
- stimulating static and dynamic balance
- stimulating running, jumping
- stimulating fine motor control, especially the fingers and the grasp
- stimulating eye–hand coordination.

STIMULATING COGNITIVE DEVELOPMENT

Setting this objective can easily lead to misunderstandings as to what the starting point was intended to be. First of all, acceptance of the individuality of the person with a developmental disability remains a given, and no attempt is made to make the client less developmentally disabled. If the team judges it to be possible and desirable to appeal more to the client's cognitive qualities, then the music therapist can make some contributions to this. His action is not geared towards increasing traditional intelligence, but towards stimulating cognitive qualities, which will put the client in a better position to hold his own in his community. Illustrations of these types of objective include:

- learning to listen, learning to pay attention
- practising long- and short-term memory
- learning and handling concepts, such as days of the week, the meaning of words, and the like
- learning and handling a symbolic language, such as, for example, a musical notation system
- stimulating strategic forms of goal-oriented action.

In an atmosphere imposing conditions, it is possible to attempt to increase concentration. Being able to hold one's attention is actually an important condition to being able to remember, learn and act in a goal-oriented way.

What techniques are used to stimulate motor and cognitive skills?

Pascal, Gerry and Tim did not seem to pay much attention to one another. Gerry and Tim already knew the music therapist, as he used to sing with them all in the community for half-an-hour each week. During the session they were certainly together in the music room with the music therapist and the group leader; however, each one seemed to be in a world of his own. The music therapist bore in mind that, for the time being, no change would come about. In this group treatment, it was above all the individual treatment of each member of the group which would be of prime importance. The group leader and he used to sing an opening song which they repeated every session. The fact that the members of the group seemed to be experiencing no communality did not actually mean that this aspect would be neglected. During the whole of the treatment they emphasised each other's presence by naming each person by his name and by always addressing each member of the group personally, whenever they did something together.

At the beginning, the music therapist filled the sessions mainly by singing himself and making music. The group members did not have to be active in this way themselves and could, first of all, become familiar with the new situation. This produced hardly any visible, spontaneous reactions. Following this initiation period, their own first activity was asked of them using a song, the music of which was played to them: the song 'If you're happy and you know it, clap your hands' was always finished on the 'bang' when one of the group members tapped on the cymbal. The technique of the arm falling with the drum stick onto the stationary cymbal was gradually acknowledged by Pascal. Many variations of this were used for some weeks. Gradually, the hitting movement became an individual movement for Pascal. Even his palsied right hand seemed to be able to make the falling movement, within certain limitations. Support from the elbow did seem necessary to do this. As time went on, the music therapist tried to get both hands to come into contact with one another by carrying out types of clapping games. The first approach was the song 'clap your hands...' His hands were first of all continually moved in the right direction by the music therapist or the group leader and gradually the support was taken away.

The music therapist devoted a relatively large amount of attention to developing his general motor control, but his speech was also tackled at each session. This was initially done by singing: Pascal and the two others listened to the music therapist and the group leader singing the words, and retained individual words, which became audible and visible in Pascal's murmuring mouth movements, always at a certain point in a song. His speech was activated by working on his breathing. One of the types of games was that all three of them got a blowpipe (electrical pipes) with which they were able to move a ping pong ball on a large stationary drum. In this way breathing was controlled more consciously. Another technique consisted of increasing Pascal's experience of his throat sounds. With the help of a microphone and an amplifier, the music therapist attempted to make him aware of the fact that he could make sounds himself. When, through his facial expressions, he showed that he recognised that there was a relationship between himself and the sounds he was hearing, different vowels and consonants, hissing, humming, and so forth were also made, together with the sounds.

Pascal had been in the motor control group for nine months now. There were noticeable changes in his motor control and in his use of sounds. It was clear that he had not yet reached the ceiling of his abilities, but further possibilities were difficult to assess. For the time being, it was decided in the team conference that Pascal ought to continue to take part in the motor control group.

In Pascal's treatment, music-making became the principal means for developing certain aspects of his motor control. Music-making had, with the exception of singing, become fragmented: isolated sounds were being made. The choice of instruments was especially determined by the amount of motor control which was required to play them, but was also based on sound. One strike on the cymbal was more inviting, for Pascal to repeat the strike, than the sound of a wooden block. Another characteristic of motor-oriented techniques is the use of non-musical tools. When doing this, you can think of Pascal's blowpipe, but also of hoops, balls, pieces of cord, and so forth. An active use of the working space plays an important role in this objective.

TECHNIQUES ORIENTED TOWARDS BODILY AWARENESS

With Pascal, bodily awareness was only an indirect issue: a drum stick in his hand, with which to strike, doubtless drew Pascal's attention to the presence of his hand and arm, but practising motor skills did actually seem to be the most important starting point for the therapist. It has already been put forward in the discussion of the objectives that, in working on bodily awareness, we must not lose sight of aspects of developmental psychology. The basis for each person's development is experiencing your own body by means of the (tactile) senses. It is at this point that the first step lies in developing bodily awareness. The fact that sound consists of (perceptible) vibrations, is exploited in remedial music-making. Examples of how the body and vibrations can be used include: holding a resounding instrument such as a tambourine against part of the body, 'cheek-to-cheek' singing by the music therapist or lying on a sound box which has been placed between two pianos.

The next step is to familiarize the client with the different parts of his body and to make him aware of the structure of his body. The lovely thing about children's songs which are about parts of the body, whether sung about or pointed out, follows on directly from this. Wim ter Burg (1986) also describes techniques which are geared towards gaining awareness of parts of the body. One example of this is the technique where clients stand in a row and hold two ropes with both hands; the music therapist and a group leader hold the two ends tight and move the rope. The movement which the arm has to make draws the client's attention to his arms. So far, in each case an attempt is being made at getting through to him that he has a body and which the different parts are, for him to distinguish between.

After this, the aim is to show him that the different parts of his body also have different capabilities. When the main starting point for the music therapist is to develop bodily awareness, he particularly works at strengthening the movements made by the client himself.

Examples of these types of techniques are:

- moving freely to music (possibly made up by himself)
- adding to a song which is played or sung by the therapist (for example 'The cat and the fiddle')
- moving in keeping with a theme (running like different kinds of animals)
- moving on a big inflatable mattress.

The movement assignments can be extremely individual, but collective movement also contributes to a greater bodily awareness. In any case, the types of games are structured in such a way that the client experiences his body in a positive way and develops positive bodily feeling. The client can be given great satisfaction, particularly by making a moving product, such as a fantasy game with music made up themselves and movements thought up themselves. Many types of game are used in which set movements are prescribed to recognise the movement capabilities of the body. These will now be discussed.

TECHNIQUES FOR DEVELOPING MOTOR SKILLS

Pascal's treatment is a typical example of the type of remedial music-making in which practising motor skills is of prime importance. In his case, bodily control is aimed at, to acquire a command of his motor apparatus. Many music therapists find that music and movement fit together well and that the motor control is developed in different ways. Examples of movement-oriented techniques, in which music-making plays a central role, include clients playing along on percussion instruments with music made up by the therapist, or learning to play an instrument in order to develop certain motor skills. An attempt is made at improving the coordination of the different senses through music-making.

The more specific are the movements which are practised, the more music-making, actively done oneself, is, on the whole, pushed into the background. If music is already actively being made, the music therapist then continues to support the movements. Learning new movements usually occurs by means of imitation: the therapist demonstrates a movement which the clients copy. Instead of letting them freely move to music, the therapist now prescribes set movements to them. He lets them move, for example, like different animals, but also gives them practical exercises such as running to a rhythm, jumping with hoops, relaxation exercises and folk dances. The use of non-musical tools such as ropes and balls often occupies an important place in this. It should be noted that the boundary between movement therapy and remedial music-making in these kinds of exercises is being advanced more and more.

SPEECH-ORIENTED TECHNIQUES

In Pascal's therapy, one important objective was to improve his speech. The therapist's points for consideration were, particularly, assisting respiration and imitating sounds. Movement in both music therapy and movement therapy overlap to a large extent, and so speech therapy and speech-oriented techniques, to some extent, cover the same areas in remedial music-making. However, the music therapist can make a specific contribution to speech-oriented techniques.

The scope of his work is particularly based on the components of music which also have a role to play in speech: melody, rhythm, tempo, dynamics and pitch. Making music, both using instruments and singing, for and with the client, activates his sense of hearing. Yet stimulating the use of the voice will be a particularly obvious choice. By imitating detached sounds made by the music therapist, the client also discovers differences in pitch. The basis for developing speech lies in encouraging the imitation of sounds. From her experience of child rehabilitation, De Bruijn (1984) describes the way in which it is in particular flowing, continuous movements from tunes which children take in as being real. Often they can, to their own surprise, keep up with the singing with a good sense of timing. Without noticing it, rhythm, timing and dynamics are experienced and learnt.

In Pascal's case, another element was added, namely, working at a basis for developing speech: assisting respiration. To achieve this, different techniques were used, such as the technique described with the blowpipe, but also playing a wind instrument results in improving respiration and controlling respiration. At the same time, some therapists propound the idea that remedial music-making contributes to language development. Singing songs can enlarge the client's passive and active vocabulary. This is indeed the case, but the question is whether language development does not rather belong to the sphere of activity of the speech therapist.

TECHNIQUES FOR STIMULATING COGNITIVE DEVELOPMENT

In discussing objectives, increasing the concentration was given as a condition for making the stimulation of cognitive development possible. The former of these objectives is, in its turn, closely linked to the objective of learning to listen. Adriaansz and Stijlen (1986) have described how such an objective can be attained in phases. At the beginning, the difference between silence and sound plays a central role. This distinction is made tangible by alternating between silence, in reaction to a sound signal, and making noise oneself (individually or in the group). A cymbal is a captivating instrument for making the signal. Its slowly fading sound demands concerted attention and concentration. In the second phase, noises and sounds are given with an increasingly greater differentiation, and discriminating between sounds is a foremost consideration. A suitable approach can be increasing the resounding noises of a number of instruments outside the client's field of vision. Varying the sound and increasing the number of instruments calls for selective listening and increased concentration. In the closing phase, the therapist works towards playing together, so that the acquired attentive skills can be perpetuated in interacting with other people.

To stimulate the memory and the use of symbols, notation for group improvisation is created, for example. In doing so, first of all the therapist appeals to the individual's capacity for remembering the rough outline of a group improvisation session: 'When did it get louder and softer? Who played at the same time? or was it one after another? Did the music become happy or sad?' Depicting the musical movements on a large sheet of paper, with symbols thought up oneself, appeals to one's capacity for symbolising one's experiences. The fact that an improvisation session can now be repeated as a rough outline, again appeals to one's imagination and attention. Learning to play an instrument can also stimulate the development in the use of symbols and attention. The use of a colour notation system is sometimes very helpful and stimulating for the client.

If we were to compare group improvisation with the use of a colour notation system, it would once again become clear that these are fundamentally different approaches. In the case of the first of these, formative impulses are taken in, from which the client strengthens himself, whereas in learning an instrument with the help of a colour notation system means that form is attained from the outside. Both alternatives can be meaningful at different times and from different approaches.

CHAPTER FIVE

Conclusion

This short final chapter is reflective in character. In the four previous chapters we have dealt with various points of view concerning care through the medium of music-making, and practical methods have been described. In this chapter, individual critical observations of the methods which have been sketched, and conclusions from the research on which this book is based, are made. Individual theoretical conclusions are also drawn and a glimpse into the future is taken.

What theoretical conclusions can be drawn from this study?

Product and process

In the description of the four methods, time and again it came up for discussion how both product-oriented work and process-oriented work is carried out with the help of music. It was also put forward in Chapter Two, on the basis of theoretical considerations that, in music therapy, orientation towards the process is more important, whilst with remedial music-making the realization of both a product and a process can be pursued. Whoever is practically engaged in working with people with developmental disabilities will discover how making a concrete musical product can be of great value to the client. Once again, we will come back to the difference between product- and process-orientation.

In looking at the methods of music therapy for individual treatment, it comes to our attention how working in a product-oriented way is avoided in favour of working in a process-oriented way. This is made apparent, amongst a number of other ways, by using interactional techniques and techniques which affect the handling of the therapeutic relationship. Conversely, learning musical techniques is expressly to be avoided. That means that a music therapist will want to conduct the courses of process therapy being in a position both to supervise a musical process, and to handle the therapeutic relationship.

With two other methods, which are both types of remedial music-making, working in a product-oriented way appears to be combined with working in a process-oriented way. This is, in fact, the case with the methods for individual remedial music-making and with the methods for the group stimulation of social skills. The two-sided nature of this is illustrated in the fact that both the techniques of 'learning musical skills' and 'carrying out a project in a process-oriented way' are used. In other words, although the therapist and the client are clear as to what the desired end product might be, the therapist will endeavour to find room for each person's individual input in the activity and, in doing so, adjust his planning accordingly. It is also possible to initiate a process of change in the client on this level by working on the realization of a musical product. In the more practical methods for motor and cognitive skills, the process–product distinction hardly plays any role. In this instance, music is what learning is wrapped up in, to such an extent that the desired end product can hardly ever be accounted for in musical terms, if at all.

It is interesting here to point out one result in the study, which up to now has not been mentioned. In Chapter Two, a theoretical definition was given of a third level of working: musical activity. By analyzing the answers of the music therapists who participated in the study on which this book is based, it did not seem possible to formulate any unequivocal method on the level of musical activities. What did stand out was that the music therapists who said they were working in that way emphatically stated that they were working in a product-oriented way. Techniques such as 'carrying out a project in process-oriented way' or 'increasing the clients' initiative', and techniques affecting the therapeutic relationship, they said they hardly ever used, if at all.

Handling music and the role of style

There is no doubt that the medium of music plays a central role in care. It is interesting to pause to look at the characteristic ways in which the handling of music takes place in music therapy and remedial music-making.

In music therapy, the compilation of techniques is again and again an offer which is specially tailored for the client. On what does the therapist base his thinking? An important basic principle in music therapy is that the musical tools put the client in a position to be able to arrive at an individual, unique style. At the same time, the music therapist presupposes that, as he goes on with the therapy, a process of change is initiated, which will become visible in a changing style. The choice of techniques, instruments, and the way in which the therapist handles the music, are mainly based on his interpretation of the client's musical personality. The term, musical personality, needs some explanation. Just as every person has their own, characteristic handwriting or way of talking, similarly, the way in which someone gives shape to his musical world is also extremely characteristic of the person. The music therapist considers the musical style, which is characteristic of the other person's view, or his needs. The music therapist endeavours to find a point of contact with this and consequently to set a process of change in motion. Sometimes the musical style, which comes about as a result of musical processes, does not mesh with the style which the client has in mind. The music therapist will then have to weigh up which of the two he prefers to let go of at that moment. This point of view about music and personality links with the methods of music therapy which are taught at the Nijmegen College of Higher Education.

The above considerations as regards the break-down of the musical process, the therapeutic process and the style, are all, essentially, suppositions. It would be interesting to investigate whether the musical process is actually a reflection of a psychic process, and when the two processes, running parallel with one another, conflict with one another.

With remedial music-making, the handling of music is a mixture of style, specific to the person, and product-orientation. This mainly applies for the methods in individual remedial music-making and for group methods, in which social skills are developed. In this instance too, the therapeutic and the musical processes can definitely be combined. However, because arriving at a product is an objective in techniques such as learning to play an instrument or working in the light of a project, the therapist will, indeed, intervene even when it is not in keeping with his interpretation of the musical and thera-peutic process.

With the group method, in which motor and cognitive skills are stimulated, considerations about the musical or the therapeutic proc-ess are almost absent. This is closely linked to the fact that music is mainly used in this instance to wrap up the learning and practising of skills. Especially when the development of motor skills is being pursued, the impression gained from the final stage in the motor control will form the basis for the choice of techniques and instru-ments. Also, in developing skills such as concentration, listening, forming ideas and the like, the concrete final objective is the thera-pist's guideline. Musical or therapeutic processes are in that case of less and less importance.

The fact that the course of these methods runs in phases, speaks for itself. What is more, even if the therapist leaves the aspect of process to one side, he should in any case give his attention to providing a course of treatment in phases.

The relationship between music therapy, remedial music-making and musical activities

It was pointed out in Chapter Two that an important characteristic of acting methodically is that the therapist acts with direction and control. That is to say, he starts from some basic assumptions which are, in fact, choices concerned with how meaningfully to use (contra-)indications, objectives, techniques and instruments. We will now pause briefly to deal with the relationship between two different possible choices, namely the choice in favour of an individual or a group approach and the choice in favour of a method using music therapy, remedial music-making or musical activities. Let us take as the therapist's basic assumption the fact that he accommodates for the emotional problems of the client in the treatment. The relationship between methodical choices can be reproduced according to the diagram on page 99.

On the horizontal axis of the diagram, the extent to which the therapist accommodates for the client's emotional problems in the treatment is shown, whilst on the vertical axis, the type of care and the method of working are represented.

In the bottom left hand corner of the diagram it can be seen how group musical activities fit together when accommodating for the client's emotional problems. If that is the case, the objectives which the therapist pursues are not specific to the person: in a group, one activity is offered from which the client can derive a sense of pleasure and in which he can participate, if he so chooses. The fact that he is able, at the same time, to develop more self-confidence by making music is a welcomed by-product of the activity. How the therapist accommodates for the client's emotional problems in the treatment is fairly arbitrary. All the same, each musical activity which provides the participant with pleasure, fulfils the requirement which the therapist makes in choosing his techniques.

Diagram

If we look at the relationship between remedial music-making and how the client's emotional problems are accommodated for, we can establish that, in contrast to the level of the musical activities, remedial music-making strives after controlled change. With the group methods for developing motor and cognitive skills, the client's individual problems do not, however, play a central role, but rather the practical skills which he has to learn. With the group methods for developing social skills, on the other hand, the client's emotional capacity does play a central role, since the individual problems, which the client may encounter in communicating with others, are worked on in order to achieve this. With individual remedial music-making, action is probably extremely controlled and specific for each person, but the objectives are usually relatively arbitrary, such as aiming for growth, achieving expression, and the like.

At the top right hand corner of the diagram, we see that the greatest amount of accommodation for the client's emotional problems takes place with individual music therapy. The controlled changes which the therapist aims to bring about particularly concern the client's psychological problems and, in the course of the therapy, his emotional experience plays a central role.

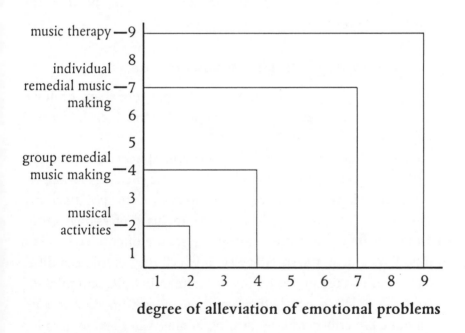

Figure 1 The correlation between the type of activity and the degree of alleviation of the client's emotional problems

To qualify what has been said thus far

The results of the study are a random indication

Virtually every music therapist who has studied the four methods will react that he too works in this way, but will assert that an infinite number of variations on these themes is possible. It remains, of course, a limitation of the study that the descriptions of the methods are based on a cross-section of music therapists' practice. The music therapists did indeed give an answer to the question: 'Could you please tell me how you are working with your client at the moment?' No answer, however, came out of the study in response to the question as to which adjustments the music therapist makes with certain clients or in which phase of the treatment he uses different techniques. In practice, the methods outlined will, however, be identified as basic patterns.

Every institution is different; no two clients are the same

An important qualification to the text in the previous chapter follows from the fact that there is not a single institution which is identical to any other.

Each institution has an individual atmosphere for treatment, which, to a great extent, determines the music therapist's room for manoeuvre. He will, in any case, have to start at this point and can subsequently endeavour to give shape to his professional action within this framework. Although processes are often identical in a form of treatment, the specific way in which they unfold can differ greatly. For this reason, collecting concrete techniques and thinking about the order in which they come in process-oriented therapy cannot be prescribed without bearing in mind the client in question and working with him. That is why in this book 'recipes' are avoided.

There are differences in the methods used between a child day care centre,
an adult day care centre and a residential unit

In the previous two chapters, four methods were outlined: two for individual, and two for group treatment. Virtually nowhere in these chapters did we pause to deal with the differences which arise from the sort of institution where music therapists work (or from the client's level of functioning). The fact that this has not happened up to now is to do with an important fact which came out of the study. Roughly speaking, most music therapists appear to use these four methodical approaches (or a number of them). How preferable they may be for one particular method, however, differs somewhat from one institution to another. Making statements about the differences in practice between a child day care centre, adult day care centre or residential unit is difficult. Within these groups there are also very divergent ideas about approaches towards treatment. That is why the word 'seems' appears on so many occasions.

If, first of all, we examine more closely the two methods for individual treatment, then there seems to be unequivocal differences, both concerning the indications and the objectives. On the whole, it is the case that music therapists in an adult day care centre seem to find consideration of the indications and objectives less important than do their colleagues in a child day care centre or a residential unit.

These differences are probably determined by differing approaches towards treatment by music therapists in the three institutions. In a child day care centre, where work is conducted with children, working in a way oriented towards the child's future (and therefore his treatment) plays a relatively central role. In an institution, there is, essentially, only a referral to the department of music therapy if there is a clear reason for offering treatment. The music therapist's ideas about treatment will, in both environments, consist explicitly of 'planned action'. The situation in an adult day care centre differs in this respect, because there is a continuous daytime intake. Hence, it is logical that a lot of attention is devoted towards care in the form of musical activities within the framework of stimulating clients and letting them spend the day there, besides offering planned treatment. Sometimes music therapists also use individual forms of treatment to teach musical skills. Making recommendations for music therapy and, to a lesser extent, setting objectives, plays a secondary role in this.

In the Netherlands on a national level, as regards the adult day care centres within the regions at present, there is a tendency towards differentiating between professional care, activity-oriented care and more treatment-oriented care. If this process is put into effect, the differences which have now been established between a child day care centre and residential unit on the one hand and a adult day care centre on the other, will in the future probably be traceable back to differences between adult day care centres themselves.

Whenever we compare indications, contra-indications and objectives of the two methods for group treatment, a different picture emerges from that for the methods for individual treatment. Particularly in a residential unit, a hostile attitude in the client towards music gives the music therapist an important reason for not offering group treatment. At adult day care centres, this plays a lesser role, but on the whole this is not the case at child day care centres. One obvious explanation for this is that the children's attitudes towards music are not yet very pronounced. For many children, music constitutes an invitation which they take up without any reticence. With adults, their attitude is often more cut and dried. If we look at the indications and the objectives, music therapists in child day care centres appear to hold more store by these kinds of considerations than those in adult day care centres and institutions. This is predominantly the case concerning objectives which aim to stimulate motor and cognitive skills. Group treatment is incorporated after more consideration in child day care centres than in adult day care centres or institutions. However, therapists tend to differ less from one another than is the case in individual treatment. We can also establish the fact that, on the subject of indications and objectives for group treatment, there is a great deal of unanimity between therapists in the various institutions.

As for their use of techniques, there are clear differences between therapists. Music therapists at child day care centres have more preference for techniques with which body-oriented work is carried out, such as developing bodily awareness and improving motor control. The techniques are often carried out in a group, but they are intended more for the individual. The therapist is musically active himself and plays or sings for the clients. Opting for a group is, in fact, useful for treating several clients at the same time. At adult day care centres, techniques such as making music together (possibly learning musical skills), working towards a project or themes, and working on a project in a process-oriented way, play a more central role. Choosing a group in this instance is, consequently, combined with using the group as a working medium to promote interaction between clients. Music therapists in residential institutions, however, appear not to have pronounced preferences for particular techniques.

Roughly speaking, it can be suggested that the type of the care which is known as 'musical activities', having hardly been touched on in the discussion of methods, is used disproportionately in the three different institutions. Music therapists appear to work more often at adult day care centres with musical activities, than those in the residential institutions and the child day care centres. This probably is linked with their training: therapists working at adult day care centres tend to have been trained at a conservatory, whereas relatively more therapists who work at child day care centres and in residential institutions have a music therapy training from one of the four acknowledged courses for music therapy.

An overview

Music therapy in caring for people with a developmental disability

An important development in caring for people with developmental disabilities is the increasing recognition of their psychological problems and the necessity for treatment. On the whole, the assertion can be made that, traditionally, more attention has been devoted to the psychological problems of people with developmental disabilities in institutions and at child day care centres than at adult day care centres. Particularly in institutions, the favoured approach to treatment has mainly been behavioural therapy. With ever-mounting interest in psychological problems, the need is also emerging to develop effective methods in psychotherapy. It is our opinion that the methods of music therapy, which have been outlined in this book, can be a valuable type of psychotherapeutic care for people with developmental disabilities. Further research will probably result in assertions about the actual efficiency of music therapy.

Particularly at adult day care centres, the time needed to develop this type of care seems, however, to be the mitigating factor. More and more, the point of view is held (once again), that a person with a developmental disability should spend as much of the day as possible in their day time group. With this philosophy, any possible help for psychological problems cannot go beyond the bounds of (group) remedial music-making. An individual indication will then not be given and, consequently, the objectives pursued are not as specific to the client. Moreover, the choice of techniques is then probably determined on the whole by the group objectives rather than the client's emotional needs. From the point of view of psychotherapeutic care for people with developmental disabilities, this kind of one-sided emphasis of working in a group-oriented way is definitely undesirable.

Remedial music-making and types of training

In the last few years, the term 'music therapy' has come under increasing pressure. Until recently, the term was used as a generic term, covering many different methods. Emerging particularly out of the context of care for people with developmental disabilities, attempts have recently been made at arriving at a better definition. Consequently, the term 'educational music therapy' has been introduced by Kemmelmejer and Probst in Dortmund (West Germany). This is a confusing term, as 'educational' and 'therapeutic' are bracketed together as a result. At the Rotterdam Conservatory a specialist course has been offered for a number of years under the name 'remedial music-making'. In 1986 there was a report on the project, in which a statement was given on research into the opinions of care workers from various professional groups as to the theoretical substance of remedial educational music-making. One of the conclusions of the report was that one sphere of activity has to be clarified, so that remedial educational music-making can be used. On the basis of this report a four year training course was started in Maastricht in 1987. Besides the term 'music therapy', the term 'remedial (educational) music-making' is consequently finding more and more acceptance with practitioners of this profession (at least, as represented by the Dutch training colleges).

The continuing clarification of the term might be of great significance for subsequent developments in the care given to people with developmental disabilities through the medium of music. The various methods can, in theory, be distinguished from one another more clearly, to promote the availability of knowledge and training. In the Netherlands there are three different sorts of training after which graduates are able to call themselves music therapists: a training course at one of the three schools for creative therapy, a training course combining the HBO-J and the Maastricht Conservatory, and specialist courses at conservatories. The training courses' fight for survival, given today's cut-backs, will probably result in there being a greater theoretical depth and responsibility, which might be looked upon as a by-product, which was not obtained methodically through controlled action, but is still highly desirable. Research is also becoming a possibility, as it is becoming clearer what areas ought to be researched. However, the disadvantages of emphasising differences in method, which might well be serious, do stick.

First of all, the importance of the image of music therapists in relation to the outside world may not become any more distinct. The introduction of remedial music-making alongside music therapy could be confusing for those who are not music therapists. The general picture that exists about music therapy is so vague at the moment that the process of theoretical refining only serves to interrupt a consistent representation of the possibilities and limitations of the 'subject'. It is our opinion that, in any case, when talking about caring for people with developmental disabilities, music therapy and remedial music-making are elements of the same subject. The fact that there are different training courses in the Netherlands, each of which provides training for a part of this subject, is not a good thing from this point of view. The fact that there are different training courses can be understood from the history of the training institutes in music therapy. For a long time they did not recognise the area of remedial music-making and consequently did not offer any training in it. On the basis of the research, conducted by us, it has not been possible to make any scientifically-founded statement over the desirability of two possibilities for training. In any case, it is such that fragmentation and cohesion is not what is called for to represent the subject.

Professionalisation and professional associations in the Netherlands

Discussing the training situation in the Netherlands brings us to our last subject: the break-down of the group, music therapists. In the short description of the history of caring for people with developmental disabilities through the medium of music, it became clear that a lot of pioneering work has been done by therapists who do not have an adequate training, such as might be acquired at a conservatory. There are three acknowledged training courses for music therapy (the so-called Mikojel-Schools), but they have not produced any graduates until relatively recently. Consequently, a current breakdown of this occupational group consists largely (about three-quarters) of music therapists without any training in creative therapy.

It is probable that the register established in 1987 by the Dutch Association for Creative Therapy, intended for creative therapists (including music therapists), will bring about a change in the breakdown of this professional body. One of the reasons for introducing this kind of register is to describe the professional identity of the music therapist more closely. It is particularly the criteria which have been developed for being included in the register which will influence the future identity of registered music therapists. In any case, as a result of this, more justice will be done to the specific expertise of the music therapist. Worthy of recommendation is the fact that institutions for people with developmental disabilities should break new ground by making their selection requirement from the point of view of qualitative supervision, before registering music therapists.

Appendix 1

The research methods

An important basic principle of the study on which this book was based was the fact that caring for people with a developmental disability through the medium of music-making is a subject which has only been practised for a relatively short time. Consequently, although information about practical experience is available from those who are practising, this experience has not yet been described systematically and thus remains limited to the knowledge of individual music therapists. In order to make the experience of music therapists available to others, in the course of the study a large number of music therapists were questioned as to their working methods. The objective was to collate and analyze the practical experience of music therapists, in order to give some structure to the available methods.

Readers of the literature on music therapy will know that a great variety of working methods has been put together under this heading. To create theoretical clarity (before asking the advice of the music therapist himself), we needed first to formulate theoretical definitions of the different terms which refer to ways of working with music (these are set out in Chapter Two). A first impression of various working methods was attained by comprehensively questioning six music therapists about their working methods. To do this a decision-theory research methodology was used. Central questions in the discussions were 'What are the (contra-)indications and objectives?' and 'With the help of which techniques and which instruments do you think a particular objective can best be attained?' A second approach towards this subject was to study literature about music therapy.

A study of the literature and discussion with the six music therapists suggested a broad range of different working methods. All the small pieces of fairly incohesive information were subsequently formed into a questionnaire. This questionnaire was sent out to music therapists working in three categories of institution: child day care centres,[1] adult day care centres and institutions for people with developmental disabilities in the Netherlands. Virtually all the institutions for people with developmental disabilities were telephoned, to be asked whether a music therapist was working on their staff. A hundred and twelve people, that is, 77 per cent of the music therapists who were asked to take part, returned a completed copy of the questionnaire. The distribution of the questionnaires throughout the various institutions appeared to be ideal; there was a diverse range of institutes represented and the proportion of men and women was equally balanced. The break-down of the group of music therapists, who participated in the study, is a highly representative reflection of this occupational group.

In the questionnaire, 444 items have been recorded, covering the following subjects:

1. Questions about working environment and training.

2. Questions about individual therapy and group therapy:

   - ways in which the therapist offers treatment
   - indications and contra-indications
   - objectives
   - techniques
   - instruments.

The way in which the questions were asked and answered was not examined at this point. In the processing of the 112 completed questionnaires, a computer was used which, with the aid of statistical calculations, graphically represented the correlation between the

---

1   The Dutch institution 'kinderdagverblijven' has been translated throughout this book as 'child day care centres' which would include special schools and special nurseries.

answers. The anomaly of this in practical terms and the interpretations of these relationships you will find in Chapters Three and Four. Four methods are described in these chapters.

To round off the study, it was examined whether the questionnaire, used in the study, was a reliable tool in assessing what music therapists actually do in practice. Participants in the study were asked to provide video recordings of music therapy sessions. Using the questionnaire, four experienced music therapists assessed eighteen excerpts of therapy as to the objectives pursued and the techniques employed. They appeared to be in full agreement with one another and even to arrive at the same evaluation as the music therapists, who assessed their own excerpts. On the basis of this it can be concluded that the reliability of the questionnaire is acceptable, at least in examining objectives and techniques.

Bibliography

Adriaansz, R. and Stijlen, L. (1986) Muziektherapie in de zorg voor volwassen verstandelijk gehandicapten. In R. Adriaansz, F. Schalkwijk and L. Stijlen (eds) *Methoden van Muziektherapie.* Nijkerk: Intro.

Alvin, J. (1965) *Music for the Handicapped Child.* London: Oxford University Press.

Alvin, J. (1966) *Music Therapy.* London: John Clare Books.

Berghs, J.H.M., Habets, A.J.C., Heilbron, B.M. and Rademakers, J.W.B.A. (1986) *Eindverslag project 'Orthopedagogisch muziekbeofenaar'.* Maastricht.

Beugen, M. van, (1986) *Sociale technologie en het instrumentale karakter van agogische actie.* Assen: Van Gorcum.

Blatter, R.P., van Nunen, P. and Verhoeven, J. (1982) *De muziek waard.* Den Haag: Nijgh and van Ditmar.

Boxill, E. (1985) *Music Therapy for the Developmentally Disabled.* Rockville: Aspen Publications.

Bruijn, M. de, (1984) *Muziek in de kinderrevalidatie.* Nijkerk: Intro.

Burg, W. ter, (1986) *Meer met muziek.* Nijkerk: Intro.

Cluckers, G., Mejkens, S., Monthaye, M., Smis, W. and Verscheuren, R. (1986) *Steungevende kinderpsychotherapie.* Deventer: Van Loghum Slaterus.

Decker-Voigt, H.H. (1975) *Musik als Lebenshilfe.* (A and B) Lilienthal/Bremen: Eres Verlag.

Dille-de Herdt, G. and Bastiaanse, M. (1985) *Creatief omgaan met muzikale expressievormen.* Antwerpen: Standaard Educatieve Uitgeverij.

Dosen, A. (1983) *Psychische stoornisse bij zwakzinninge kinderen.* Lisse: Swets and Zeitlinger.

Fockema-Andreae, L. (1986) Muziektherapeutische observatie. In R. Adriaansz, F. Schalkwijk and L. Stijlen (eds) *Methoden van Muziektherapie.* Nijkerk: Intro.

Grabau, E. and Visser, H. (eds) (1987) *Creatieve Therapie.* Deventer: Van Loghum Slaterus.

Kemmelmejer, K.J. and Probst, W. (1981) *Quellentexte zur paedagoggischen Muziektherapie.* Regensburg: G. Bosse Verlag.

Kugel, J. (1973) *Psychologie van het lichaam.* Utrecht: Aula pockets.

Lecourt, E. (1980) *La Pratique de la musicotherapie.* Paris: E.S.F.

Lievegoed, B. (1939) *Maat, ritme en melodie.* Zeist: Uitgeverij Vrij Geestesleven.

Nordoff, P. and Robbins, C. (1971) *Music Therapy in Special Education.* New York: John Day.

Rest, E. van, (1986) Muziektherapie op een kinderdagverblijf. In R. Adriaansa, F. Schalkwijk and L. Stijlen (eds) *Methoden van Muziektherapie.* Nijkerk: Intro.

Rider, M.S. (1981) The assessment of cognitive functionning level through musical perception. *Journal of Music Therapy, 18,* 110–119.

Schalkwijk, F.W. (1984) *Grondslagen van muziektherapie.* Nijmegen: Dekker and van de Vegt.

Stijlen, L. (1984) In F.W. Schalkwijk *Grondslagen van muziektherapie.* Nijmegen: Dekker and van de Vegt.

Wijck, I. van and Hulsegge, H. (1985) *Spelend omgaan met muziek.* Nijkerk: Intro.

Introduction to Dramatherapy
Sue Jennings
ISBN 1 85302 115 6 pb

Persona and Performance
The Meaning of Role in Drama, Therapy and Everyday Life
Robert J Landy
ISBN 1 85302 229 2 hb

Art Therapy with Offenders
Edited by Marian Liebmann
ISBN 1 85302 171 7 pb

Music Therapy in Health and Education
Edited by Margaret Heal and Tony Wigram
Foreword by Anthony Storr
ISBN 1 85302 175 X pb

Play Therapy with Abused Children
Ann Cattanach
ISBN 1 85302 193 8 pb
ISBN 1 85302 120 2 hb

Play Therapy
Where the Sky Meets the Underworld
ISBN 1 85302 250 0 hb
ISBN 1 85302 211 X pb

Post Traumatic Stress Disorder and Dramatherapy
Treatment and Risk Reduction
Linda Winn
ISBN 1 85302 183 0 pb

Chain Reaction
Children and Divorce
Ofra Ayalon and Adina Flasher
ISBN 1 85302 136 9 pb

Jessica Kingsley Publishers
116 Pentonville Road, London. N1 9JB
Tel: 071-833-2307 Fax: 071-837-2917

Art Therapy and Dramatherapy
Masks of the Soul
Sue Jennings and Åse Minde
ISBN 1 85302 027 3 hb

Handbook of Inquiry in the Arts Therapies
One River, Many Currents
Edited by Helen Payne
Foreword by John Rowan
1993 276 pages, illus ISBN 1 85302 153 9 pb £19.95

Movement and Drama in Therapy 2nd edition
A Holistic Approach
Audrey G Wethered
Foreword by Chloë Gardner
ISBN 1 85302 199 7 pb

Symbols of the Soul
Therapy and Guidance Through Fairy Tales
Birgitte Brun, Ernst W Pedersen and Marianne Runberg
Foreword by Murray Cox
ISBN 1 85302 107 5 hb

Approaches to Case Study
A Handbook for Those Entering the Therapeutic Field
Robin Higgins
ISBN 1 85302 182 2 pb

The Metaphoric Body
Guide to Expressive Therapy through Images and Archetypes
Leah Bartal and Nira Ne'eman
Foreword by Harris Chaiklin
ISBN 1 85302 152 0 pb

Jessica Kingsley Publishers
116 Pentonville Road, London. N1 9JB
Tel: 071-833-2307 Fax: 071-837-2917

Storymaking in Bereavement
Dragons Fight in the Meadow
Alida Gersie
ISBN 1 85302 176 8 pb
ISBN 1 85302 065 6 hb

Focus on Psychodrama
The Therapeutic Aspects of Psychodrama
Peter Felix Kellermann
Foreword by Jonathan D Moreno
ISBN 1 85302 127 X pb

Dramatherapy with Families, Groups and Individuals
Waiting in the Wings
Sue Jennings
ISBN 1 85302 144 X pb
ISBN 1 85302 014 1 hb

Christian Symbols, Ancient Roots
Elizabeth Rees
Foreword by Sue Jennings
ISBN 1 85302 046 X hb

Art Therapy in Practice
Edited by Marian Liebmann
ISBN 1 85302 057 5 hb
ISBN 1 85302 058 3 pb

Drama and Healing
The Roots of Drama Therapy
Roger Grainger
ISBN 1 85302 048 6 hb

Storymaking in Education and Therapy
Alida Gersie and Nancy King
ISBN 1 85302 519 4 hb
ISBN 1 85302 520 8 pb

Jessica Kingsley Publishers
116 Pentonville Road, London. N1 9JB
Tel: 071-833-2307 Fax: 071-837-2917